V. Sackville-West

V. Sackville-West

A CRITICAL BIOGRAPHY
BY

Michael Stevens

LONDON
MICHAEL JOSEPH

First published in Great Britain by
MICHAEL JOSEPH LTD
52 Bedford Square
London, W.C.1
1973

7181 1085 4

*Printed in Great Britain by
Redwood Press Limited, Trowbridge, Wiltshire
and bound by James Burn Ltd. at Esher, Surrey*

CONTENTS

ILLUSTRATIONS

FOREWORD

V. Sackville-West is an author who does not yet appear to have received the attention that her work merits, for although her novels, biographies and poetry are widely read, little seems to have been written about her since her death in 1962. While in no way claiming that the present critical biography is complete, or even does justice to the complex personality or works of this interesting writer, it is my hope that it will contribute some information and insight which may stimulate some later biographer to write the fuller work on her which she deserves.

I should like to take this opportunity of acknowledging the debt of thanks I owe to all those who have been of assistance to me while writing this biography. My greatest debt is to Mr Nigel Nicolson, without whose unstinted aid from the very first, this work could never have been written. His generosity in placing his mother's manuscripts and other papers at my disposal, in indicating other sources, some of which, unfortunately, are not yet available, and in answering so many questions, has been invaluable.

I am also deeply indebted to Dr Marianne Beyer. She has followed the development of this book from its inception, and has not only saved me from many pitfalls, but, by reason of her wide learning, has been of great help in showing me the way to proceed. I should also like to thank Docent Bertil Johansson, who read the first draft of this work, for a great deal of shrewd comment; my advisers at Uppsala University, Professor Gunnar Boklund, Docent Gunnar Sorelius, Docent Birgit Bramsbäck and Docent Adina Forsgren, for much helpful criticism; my colleagues in Stockholm, Lektors Pamela Rees-Björnberg, Alan Dixon, Ian Dunlop and Michael Knight for their help with proof-reading. Last, but by no means least, my thanks to my wife and daughter for their patience and understanding.

Victoria Sackville-West's Major Works

Year	V S-W's age	Poetry	Fiction	Non-Fiction
1906	14		"Edward Sackville, Earl of Dorset"	
1907	15		"Le Masque de Fer"	
1907	15		"Jean-Baptiste Poquelin"	
1907	15		"The King's Secret"	
1907	15		"Richelieu"	
1909	17	*Chatterton*		
1910	18		"Alcibiades"	
1910	18		"The City of the Lily"	
1915	23	*Constantinople*		
1918	26	*Poems of West and East*		
1919	27		*Heritage*	
1921	29	*Orchard and Vineyard*		
1921	29		*The Dragon in Shallow Waters*	
1922	30			*Knole and the Sackvilles*
1922	30		*The Heir*	
1923	31		*Grey Wethers*	
1923	31			*The Diary of Lady Anne Clifford*
1923	31		*Challenge*	
1924	32		*Seducers in Ecuador*	
1926	34			*Passenger to Teheran*
1926	34	*The Land*		
1927	35			*Aphra Behn*
1928	36			*Twelve Days*
1929	37	*King's Daughter*		
1929	37			*Andrew Marvell*
1930	38		*The Edwardians*	

8

Year	V S-W's age	Poetry	Fiction	Non-Fiction
1931	39		*All Passion Spent*	
1931	39	*Sissinghurst*		
1932	40		*Family History*	
1932	40		*Thirty Clocks Strike the Hour*	
1933	41	*Collected Poems*		
1934	42		*The Dark Island*	
1936	44			*St Joan of Arc*
1937	45			*Pepita*
1938	46	*Solitude*		
1941	49	*Selected Poems*		
1942	50		*Grand Canyon*	
1943	51			*The Eagle and the Dove*
1945	53	*Another World Than This* (with H.N.)		
1946	54	*The Garden*		
1947	55		*Devil at Westease*	
1953	61		*The Easter Party*	
1959	67			*Daughter of France*
1961	69		*No Signposts in the Sea*	

A Table of Dates

9 March 1892	V. Sackville-West born at Knole.
ca. 1900	Sir John Murray Scott becomes a friend of the family.
1906	V S-W writes her first novel, "Edward Sackville, Earl of Dorset."
1907	Writes "Le Masque de Fer", "Jean-Baptiste Poquelin", "The King's Secret", and "Richelieu".
July 1907	Wins verse competition in the *Onlooker*.
Spring 1908	Accompanies her mother and Violet Keppel to Pisa and Milan.
Summer 1908	Death of V S-W's grandfather. Her parents inherit the title.
Spring 1909	Goes to Florence and Rome.
Autumn 1909	Accompanies her mother and Sir John to Poland and Russia.
Autumn 1909	*Chatterton* privately published.
Feb 1910	The law-suit to decide the succession to the title.
Spring 1910	Goes to Florence.
1910	Writes "Alcibiades" and "The City of the Lily".
Summer 1910	"Comes out", Meets Harold Nicolson at a party.
Summer 1910	Ill with pneumonia.
Autumn 1910	Spends six months with her mother at a villa near Monte Carlo to recuperate. Harold Nicolson a frequent visitor.
Spring 1911	Goes to Florence with her mother.
Autumn 1911	Harold Nicolson a frequent visitor at Knole.
Jan 1912	Sir John Murray Scott dies. V S-W and Harold Nicolson secretly engaged. Harold Nicolson leaves for Constantinople.
Aug 1912	Harold Nicolson returns from Constantinople.
Oct 1912	Goes to Italy for six months with Harold Nicolson and Rosamund Grosvenor.
Spring 1913	Goes to Spain with Rosamund Grosvenor.
June 1913	The law-suit to contest Sir John's will.
July 1913	The engagement between V S-W and Harold Nicolson made public.
1 Oct 1913	V S-W and Harold Nicolson married at Knole.
Oct 1913	Honeymoon in Italy and Egypt.
Winter 1914	The Nicolsons in Constantinople.
June 1914	Return to England.
Aug 1914	Birth of Benedict Nicolson at Knole.
Oct 1914	The Nicolsons move to London.
1915	*Constantinople* privately published.
Summer 1915	The Nicolsons purchase Long Barn, near Knole.
Jan 1917	Birth of Nigel Nicolson in London.
1917	*Poems of West and East*.
1919	*Heritage*. Harold Nicolson at the Peace Conference in Paris.
1920	Crisis in the marriage of V S-W and Harold Nicolson. Harold Nicolson returns to the Foreign Office in London.

1921	*The Dragon in Shallow Waters. Orchard and Vineyard.*
1922	*The Heir. Knole and the Sackvilles.* First meeting with Leonard and Virginia Woolf.
1923	*The Diary of Lady Anne Clifford. Grey Wethers. Challenge.* A start made on *The Land.*
1924	*Seducers in Ecuador,* written for Virginia Woolf.
1925	The bulk of *The Land* written.
Feb 1926	V S-W goes to Persia, returning in the summer via Russia.
Autumn 1926	*The Land. Passenger to Teheran.*
1927	V S-W returns to Persia and makes a journey through the Bakhtiari Mountains. H.N. transferred to Berlin. V S-W awarded the Hawthornden Prize for *The Land. Aphra Behn.*
Feb 1928	Death of Lord Sackville. Knole passes to V S-W's uncle.
1928	*Twelve Days.* Virginia Woolf publishes *Orlando.*
1929	*King's Daughter. Andrew Marvell.* Harold Nicolson receives an offer from Lord Beaverbrook and hands in his resignation to the Foreign Office. He moves into chambers in the City.
Jan 1930	Harold Nicolson joins the staff of the *Evening Standard.*
May 1930	The Nicolsons buy Sissinghurst Castle in Kent. *The Edwardians.*
1930	*Sissinghurst.*
March 1931	Harold Nicolson joins Mosley's New Party.
May 1931	*All Passion Spent.*
August 1931	Harold Nicolson resigns from the *Evening Standard* to edit *Action.*
Summer 1932	Harold Nicolson leaves the New Party and starts reviewing.
Oct 1932	*Family History. Thirty Clocks Strike the Hour.*
Jan 1933	The Nicolsons leave for a three-month lecture tour of the United States.
Autumn 1933	*Collected Poems.*
Spring 1934	V S-W and Gwen St. Aubyn in Portofino, then, with Harold Nicolson, in Morocco.
Oct 1934	*The Dark Island.*
April 1935	The Nicolsons on a cruise to Greece.
Autumn 1935	V S-W in Domrémy, Chinon and Orleans to do research for *Saint Joan of Arc,* accompanied by Gwen St. Aubyn.
Nov 1935	Harold Nicolson elected M.P. for West Leicester.
Jan 1936	Lady Sackville dies.
May 1936	*Saint Joan of Arc.*
1937	Tour of North Africa. *Pepita.* Journey with Gwen St. Aubyn to France.
1938	*Solitude.*
March 1941	Virginia Woolf commits suicide.
1942	*Grand Canyon.*
1943	*The Eagle and the Dove.* V S-W passes through a spiritual crisis.
1946	*The Garden.*
Jan 1947	V S-W makes a start on *Daughter of France.*
Feb 1947	Harold Nicolson joins the Labour Party.
June 1947	V S-W awarded the Heinemann Prize for *The Garden.*
1947	*Nursery Rhymes. Devil at Westease.*
Dec 1947	V S-W made a Companion of Honour.
Feb 1948	V S-W goes to North Africa for two months to lecture for the British Council.
March 1948	Harold Nicolson defeated in a by-election.
March 1949	V S-W goes to Spain on a lecture tour for the British Council.
1949	Becomes a Justice of the Peace, sits on the National Trust's Gardens

Committee and the Executive of the Society for the Preservation of Rural Kent.

Dec 1950	V S-W starts writing *The Easter Party*.
Jan 1953	*The Easter Party*.
March 1953	Work resumed on *Daughter of France*.
March 1955	V S-W injures her back.
Dec 1955	Steegmuller publishes his biography of La Grande Mademoiselle.
Jan 1957	The Nicolsons on a cruise to Java.
Dec 1957	On a cruise to South America.
Autumn 1958	*Daughter of France* finished.
Jan 1959	Cruise to Singapore and Saigon. *No Signposts in the Sea* begun.
March 1959	*Daughter of France* published.
Summer 1959	V S-W ill with virus pneumonia.
Jan 1960	Cruise to South Africa. Bulk of the work on *No Signposts in the Sea* done.
Summer 1960	V S-W ill.
Jan 1961	Cruise to South America. *Faces* written.
Feb 1961	*No Signposts in the Sea* published.
Jan 1962	V S-W has a hæmorrhage. Cruise to the West Indies.
March 1962	Cancer diagnosed.
2 June 1962	V S-W dies at Sissinghurst.

The footnotes in this volume are based on the system laid down by Jacques Barzun and Henry F. Graff in *The Modern Researcher*, Harcourt, Brace & Co., New York, 1957.

Victoria Sackville-West's Ancestry

Victoria Sackville-West's ancestry is somewhat unusual. On her father's side she is descended direct from Thomas Sackville, 1536—1608, later Lord Buckhurst and 1st Earl of Dorset.[1] On her mother's side she is descended from a Spanish gipsy known as Pepita.[2]

As a young man, Thomas Sackville made a reputation for himself as a poet—his contemporary, John Heywood, complimented him:

> There Sackville's sonnets sweetly sauced
> And featly finèd be.[3]

Today he is better remembered as the writer of the *Induction* to the *Mirror for Magistrates* and the *Complaint to Buckingham,* and as the co-author of *Gorboduc.* At the age of thirty, however, Thomas Sackville, who was cousin to Queen Elizabeth through the Boleyn family,[4] abandoned poetry for politics for which, by birth and by talent, he was eminently fitted. In the course of the next thirty years he was knighted,[5] created Lord Buckhurst, of Buckhurst in Sussex,[6] appointed Lord Chancellor of Oxford University[7] and, in 1599,[8] was made Lord High Treasurer of England. After the death

---

[1] For this and other genealogical information in this chapter, see *Burke's Peerage and Baronetage,* London, 1970, pp. 2333—4. See also Harold Nicolson, *Diaries and Letters, 1945—62,* London, 1968, rear inside cover-papers, where a table of descent for V. Sackville-West's immediate ancestry is to be found; also V. Sackville-West, *Knole and the Sackvilles,* London, 1922, pp. ix—xii for a chronological table of the history of Knole and the Sackville family, and pp. xiv—xv for a simplified table of the descent of the Sackvilles. Note that in this dissertation, the edition of *Knole and the Sackvilles* used is that published by Benn, London, in 1958.
For a detailed description of the Sackville family and its descent, see Phillips, *The history of the Sackville family, together with a description of Knole and the early owners of Knole,* London, 1930, Vols I and II.
[2] See Nicolson, *op. cit.,* inside rear cover-papers; *Dictionary of National Biography,* 2nd Supplement, London, 1912, p. 249; V. Sackville-West, *Pepita,* London, 1937, p. 52 ff.
[3] Quoted in *Knole and the Sackvilles,* p. 44. See also Spencer's tribute to Thomas Sackville, quoted in *D.N.B.,* L (1895), 97.
[4] Paul Bacquet, *Un contemporain d'Elisabeth I, Thomas Sackville,* Genève, 1966, is probably the leading work on Thomas Sackville. For details of the relationship between him and Queen Elizabeth, see p. 15. See also Phillips, *op. cit.,* I, 187, and *Knole and the Sackvilles,* p. 46.
[5] See Bacquet, *op. cit.,* p. 50, Phillips, *op. cit.,* I, 182, and *Knole and the Sackvilles,* p. 46.
[6] See Bacquet, *op. cit.,* p. 50, Phillips, *op. cit.,* I, 182, and *Knole and the Sackvilles,* p. 46.
[7] See Bacquet, *op. cit.,* pp. 27—8, Phillips, *op. cit.,* I, 208, and *Knole and the Sackvilles,* p. 46.
[8] *Burke's Peerage and Baronetage* appears to be wrong here. This work gives the date as 1594 (p. 2333). *Knole and the Sackvilles* gives 1599 (p. 46), as do Bacquet, *op. cit.,* p. 78 and Phillips, *op. cit.,* I, 211, both of which quote Cal. State Pap. (Dom.), Vol. CCLXX (15 May, 1599), 194 as their authority.

of Queen Elizabeth, he was confirmed in his office by James I, who elevated him to an Earldom as Earl Dorset in 1604.[9]

Apart from Thomas Sackville's poetic gifts, there are two other facts about him which are of importance when considering the life and works of V. Sackville-West (henceforth referred to as V S-W): in 1554 he married Cicely, daughter to Sir John Baker of Sissinghurst Castle in Kent,[10] and in 1556 Queen Elizabeth presented him with Knole,[11] one of the great country houses of England and, even at that time, a building of some magnificence and fame.[12]

During the reign of George I, Lionel Cranfield Sackville, 7th Earl of Dorset, was created 1st Duke of Dorset,[13] but the title was destined to die out in less than a hundred years. When the 4th Duke of Dorset died in 1815 at the age of only 21, a distant cousin succeeded to the title as 5th and last Duke. Knole, however, with all its revenues, remained the property of the Dowager Duchess, passing after her death into the hands of her daughter, Lady Elizabeth Sackville.[14] Lady Elizabeth had married in 1813 John West, 5th Earl de la Warr, by whom she had nine children: six sons and three daughters.[15] The second and third sons, Charles and Reginald Sackville-West, succeeded to their father's title, becoming the 6th and 7th Earls de la Warr. The 4th son, however, Mortimer Sackville-West, was created 1st Baron Sackville in 1876 and inherited Knole.[16] The fifth son, Lionel Sackville-West, V S-W's grandfather, was to inherit both the title and Knole upon the death of his brother in 1888.[17]

Lionel Sackville-West must have been a remarkable man in several respects. A diplomatist by profession, he was noted for his taciturnity; indeed, towards the end of his life "he was ... a queer and silent old man. ... He turned his back on all visitors, but sized them up after they had gone in one shrewd and sarcastic phrase".[18]

Yet in 1852, while on leave in Paris, he met and immediately fell in love with a twenty-two-year-old Spanish gipsy dancer known as Pepita,[19] whose life-story V S-W was later to write in the book of the same name.

Pepita, or to give her her real name, Josefa Duran y Ortega de la Oliva, is said to have been a strikingly beautiful girl for whom her ambitious mother, Catalina Ortega, had arranged dancing lessons with a view to getting her an engagement at the Teatro del Príncipe in Madrid, at that time the leading theatre in Spain.[20] The dancing lessons were a failure and Pepita's contract was cancelled,[21] but one of the male dancers at the theatre, Juan Antonio de la Oliva, had fallen violently in love with her and cancelled his own contract with the theatre in protest.[22] On 10th January, 1851, Pepita and Oliva were married, but only three months later, probably as the result of a quarrel with Catalina Ortega, Oliva walked out of the house, leaving his wife for ever.[23] Pepita left

---

[9] See Bacquet, *op. cit.,* p. 84, Phillips, *op. cit.,* I, 221, and *Knole and the Sackvilles,* p. 46.
[10] See Bacquet, *op. cit.,* p. 34, Phillips, *op. cit.,* I, 152, 239, and *Knole and the Sackvilles,* p. ix.
[11] See Phillips, *op. cit.,* II, 320, and *Knole and the Sackvilles,* p. 46.
[12] See *Knole and the Sackvilles,* pp. 21—3, and Phillips, *op. cit.,* II, 334—7.
[13] On 13th June, 1720. See *Burke,* p. 2333, Phillips, *op. cit.,* II, 14, and *Knole and the Sackvilles,* p. 159.
[14] Phillips, *op. cit.,* II, 310, and *Knole and the Sackvilles,* pp. 198—200.
[15] *Burke,* p. 2334. See also Phillips, *op. cit.,* II, 273—4, and *Knole and the Sackvilles,* p. 210.
[16] *Burke,* p. 2334. See also Phillips, *op. cit.,* II, 316—8.
[17] *Burke,* p. 2334, Phillips, *op. cit.,* II, 325, and V S-W, *Pepita.* Hogarth Press, London, 1937, p. 172.
[18] *Knole and the Sackvilles,* p. 210.
[19] *Pepita,* p. 54. For an estimate of the reliability of *Pepita* as a source of documentary evidence, see Appendix A, p. 109.
[20] *Ibid.,* pp. 23—4.
[21] *Ibid.,* p. 31.
[22] *Ibid.,* p. 31.
[23] *Ibid.,* pp. 37, 41.

Spain shortly afterwards and went to northern Europe, where, within a few months, she had made a name for herself as a Spanish dancer in Denmark, France and, in particular, in Germany as "The Star of Andalusia".[24]

From 1852, the year in which Lionel Sackville-West and Pepita first met, until 1871, when Pepita died, they lived together although they could not, of course, marry as Pepita was a Catholic and could not have obtained a divorce even if she had tried. Sackville-West's career took him all over Europe, and Pepita continued to dance until the birth of their third child in 1865, so they had to set up house in many towns: in Heidelberg, Hackenberg, Turin, Como and in Bordeaux.[25] In 1865 she settled down in a house in Arcachon, where she spent the rest of her life. She died in 1871 giving birth to a still-born son.[26]

The problem now arose as to what was to be done with the five surviving children— two boys and three girls. Sackville-West himself obviously could not look after them, particularly as he was posted to Buenos Aires as British Minister shortly after Pepita's death.[27] A temporary solution was found when a friend of Pepita's, Mme de Béon, moved into their house and looked after them there.[28] Then, in 1873, the eldest daughter, Victoria Josefa Dolores Catalina, V S-W's mother, was sent to a convent school in Paris, where she spent the following seven years. She was later joined there by her younger sisters.[29]

In 1880, when Victoria was eighteen, all the children with the exception of Maximilian, the elder son, who had been established as a farmer in South Africa,[30] were suddenly transported to England through the offices of a woman whom Lionel Sackville-West had met in Buenos Aires. There Victoria discovered that Lord de la Warr and Lord Sackville were her uncles, and that the Duchess of Bedford and the Countess of Derby were her aunts.[31] The Countess of Derby perceived that in Victoria there was material for something quite different from the governess for which she had been trained at the convent. As her brother, Lionel Sackville-West, had just been appointed British Minister in Washington, she determined to use her influence to send his illegitimate daughter with him as his hostess and mistress of his household. Though the suggestion caused consternation at first, both in British and in American circles, all opposition to the idea eventually collapsed, and in 1881 Victoria sailed for America to take charge of her father's household.[32]

She appears to have been an immediate success, for although—or perhaps partly because—she could speak English only imperfectly, and because of the great charm and beauty that she is said to have possessed, she had all Washington at her feet. It is reported that President Arthur himself made a proposal of marriage to her shortly after her arrival.[33] She refused all suitors, however, continuing to look after her father's household until, in 1888, a disaster overtook him. During the presidential election campaign of that year he was incautious enough to reply indiscreetly to a letter, purporting to

[24] *Ibid.*, pp. 49—50, 101. For further details, see the review of *Pepita* by Gustaf Stridsberg in *Svenska Dagbladet*, 13 Nov. 1938, p. 8.
[25] *Pepita*, pp. 115, 119.
[26] *Ibid.*, p. 146.
[27] *Ibid.*, p. 151.
[28] *Ibid.*, p. 151.
[29] *Ibid.*, pp. 153—4.
[30] *Ibid.*, p. 155.
[31] *Ibid.*, pp. 156—7.
[32] *Ibid.*, pp. 158—160. See also Phillips, *op. cit.*, II, 324—5 and the *DNB*, 2nd Supplement, London, 1912, p. 249.
[33] *Pepita*, p. 161.

come from a Mr Charles F. Murchison, which requested his views on the merits of the presidential candidates. The letter was published in the daily press, and the resulting public excitement was made the pretext by the American Secretary of State for declaring Sackville-West *persona non grata*.[34]

By a strange co-incidence, however, his brother, Mortimer, 1st Baron Sackville, died three weeks later, thus offering Lionel Sackville-West an opportunity of giving up his career and returning to Knole in order to administer the estate to which, with the title, he had suddenly succeeded. He was offered another important diplomatic post by Lord Salisbury, but refused it.[35]

After a few months spent in France while certain legal complications were being cleared up, Victoria took over the management of Knole for her father. She was at the time being courted by a young French marquis, but though apparently attracted by him,[36] she evidently felt that she could hardly leave her father to look after Knole by himself.[37] Just at this time of indecision she met her cousin, Lionel Sackville-West,[38] who was also the heir to the title and to Knole. He fell violently in love with her and asked her to marry him. Faced with the choice of becoming either a French marquise or an English peeress (with Knole), she eventually chose the latter; she and her cousin were married at Knole a year later, on 17th June, 1890.[39]

[34] Phillips, *op. cit.*, II, pp. 325—6, and *Pepita*, pp. 167—72. An interesting inquiry into the identity of the true author of the Murchison letter and the political situation which rendered it such an effective campaign weapon is the article by T.C. Hinckely "George Osgoodby and the Murchison Letter", Biographical footnotes, *Pacific Historical Review*, Univ. of California Press, Berkeley, XXVII (November 1958), 359—70.
The justification, or rather, lack of justification for the American Secretary of State's action in handing Lionel Sackville-West back his passport is discussed at some length in an illuminating article; "The Dismissal of Lord Sackville", C.S. Campbell jr., Biographical footnotes, *Mississippi Valley Historical Review*, XLIV (March 1958), 635—48.
[35] Phillips, *op. cit.*, II, 326.
[36] *Pepita*, pp. 176—7.
[37] *Ibid.*, p. 183.
[38] *Ibid.*, p. 184. See also *Burke*, p. 2334.
[39] *Ibid.*, pp. 184—8. See also Phillips, *op. cit.*, II, 328.

CHAPTER II

The Years 1892 to 1913

The early married life of the young Sackville-Wests appears to have been very happy. They were very much in love and they had plenty to occupy themselves with.[1] Until his death in 1908 Lord Sackville was nominally head of the household at Knole, but in fact he took no part in running it, devoting himself entirely to his own interests. Victoria, his daughter, assumed full responsibility for the house itself,[2] and Lionel, his nephew and heir, attended to the business of the estate as well as to his responsibilities as commander of the West Kent Yeomanry and his position on numerous committees in the County of Kent.

The characters of Lionel and Victoria were, however, completely different. V S-W has described her father as "the best type of English country gentleman; just, courteous, and conscientious, he was truly loved and respected by all."[3]

Victoria, on the other hand, was mercurial in the extreme. In V S-W's own words:

My mother was adorable at that time of her life. She was tiresome, of course, and wayward, and capricious, and thoroughly spoilt; but her charm and real inward gaiety enabled her to carry it all off. One forgave her everything when one heard her laugh and saw how frankly she was enjoying herself. As a child can be maddening at one moment and irresistible the next, so could my mother be maddening and irresistible by turns. For, like a child, she neither analysed nor controlled her moods: they simply blew across her,[4]

and again:

Many people have told me what a clever woman my mother was, and what good taste she had; it was a sort of label tied onto her; but it was utterly wrong. She was anything but clever, and her taste was anything but good. What they never realised was that she was, above all things, herself. Wrong or right, tiresome, troublesome, turbulent, difficult, generous, mean, vindictive, revengeful, unjust, kind, lavish, enthusiastic, all in turn, she was always herself, and to be always oneself to that extent is a form of genius.[5]

It is clear that in a marriage between two such fundamentally dissimilar personalities an open breach must come sooner or later. It was the 1914—18 war that was responsible for the final disruption. Until then they had divided their mandates at Knole fairly amicably,[6] but while Lionel, who had succeeded to the title by that time, was away in

[1] *Pepita*, p. 189.
[2] *Ibid.*, p. 183.
[3] *Ibid.*, p. 237.
[4] *Ibid.*, p. 201.
[5] *Ibid.*, p. 282.
[6] *Ibid.*, p. 255.

the Middle East and France, the only check on Lady Sackville's always autocratic character was removed, and she grew used to holding undisputed sway over the whole of Knole. When her husband returned after the war, he made it clear to her that he intended to resume control of the estate, and the resultant clash of wills led to their final separation.[7] Lady Sackville left Knole in 1919 and went to Brighton, where she had a house.[8] She never returned to her husband.

Victoria's charm and the fascination she held for other people are evident throughout the whole of the second part of *Pepita*. One of the people to fall permanently under her spell was Sir John Murray Scott,[9] whom she had met for the first time about 1900. Sir John, who was destined to become an integral part of the Sackville-West family until his death in 1912, must have been a remarkable man. Of middle-class Scottish origin, he had become secretary to Sir Richard and Lady Wallace, heirs to the property of the Marquises of Hertford and owners of the vast collection of art that is now the property of the nation—the Wallace Collection.[10] Sir Richard and Lady Wallace had grown so fond of Sir John that they had made him their heir, and on their death he inherited not only about a million pounds in cash, but also the Wallace-Hertford properties in Paris—an enormous apartment in the Boulevard des Italiens filled with art treasures—and Marie Antionette's Bagatelle in the Bois de Boulogne.[11] Sir John seems to have succumbed to Lady Sackville's charm at their very first meeting,[12] and although they were to have many violent quarrels in the years that followed, he never failed to return to her within a short time. He was frequently at Knole, and the Sackville-Wests regularly spent long periods with him in Paris or in Scotland.[13]

In 1908 Lord Sackville died,[14] and immediately a threat that had been hanging over the heads of Victoria and Lionel Sackville-West since 1896 became a reality. Victoria's brother, Henri, had claimed that Pepita's marriage to Juan Oliva was not valid and that Lionel Sackville-West (Henri and Victoria's father) had married Pepita in secret, thus making his children legitimate and Henri the rightful heir to Knole and the title. Investigations in Spain had revealed that someone had tampered with the entry in the register of the church in which Pepita and Oliva had been married, and Henri had been doing everything in his power to procure evidence to show that Lionel Sackville-West had married her.[15] Quite naturally, the press were not slow to make the most of the lawsuit that followed the death of Lord Sackville, particularly as it was necessary for Victoria to establish the fact that she was illegitimate to make it possible for her husband to succeed to the title, and for about a fortnight the Sackville-Wests lived in a blaze of publicity.[16] Eventually, Henri's case collapsed in court, and Victoria and Lionel Sackville-West returned to Knole in triumph as the rightful Lord and Lady Sackville.[17]

Two years later, in 1912, Sir John Murray Scott died, leaving to Lady Sackville a

[7] *Ibid.*, pp. 255—6.
[8] *Ibid.*, p. 257.
[9] An excellent character-sketch of Sir John Murray Scott together with some details of his life is to be found in *Pepita*, pp. 189—200.
[10] See *The Complete Peerage*, Vol VI (1926), 514 Note (a).
[11] See *The Times*, 18 January, 1912, p. 9, and *Pepita*, pp. 192—3.
[12] *Pepita*, p. 190. According to V S-W, the evening Sir John met her, "he added a codicil to his will by which he left her the sum of £50,000".
[13] *Ibid.*, pp. 189—209.
[14] See *The Times*, 4 September, 1908, p. 11.
[15] *Pepita*, pp. 213—4.
[16] The case 'Sackville-West v. West, Attorney General and others' was reported in some detail on page 3 of *The Times* on the 2nd, 3rd, 5th, 9th, 15th and 26th of February, 1910. It was frontpage news on these dates in the more sensational press.
[17] *Pepita*, pp. 211—229. When Lord and Lady Sackville reached Sevenoaks, the fire brigade took the horses out of the shafts of the victoria and drew the carriage by hand through the streets of the town right into the courtyard of Knole.

legacy of one hundred and fifty thousand pounds plus the entire contents of his apartment in Paris, valued at over a quarter of a million pounds.[18] His relatives were furious and decided to contest the will on the grounds that Lady Sackville had exercised undue influence over him. Coming as it did only a short time after the sensational lawsuit to determine the inheritance to the title, the press did not fail to exploit the case to the full. Lady Sackville was not the person to compromise by trying to obtain a settlement out of court, and after a brilliant defence in which eminent counsel were involved on both sides, she won her case.[19]

It was to these parents that V S-W was born at Knole on the 9th of March, 1892, and it was against this background that she grew up until her marriage in 1913.

Her mother (who, to avoid confusion with V S-W, will henceforth be referred to as Lady Sackville, although she did not come into the title until 1908) appears not to have been a motherly woman by temperament, but even if she had been, her responsibilities as hostess at Knole and the Edwardian conception of how children of the aristocracy should be brought up would have prevented her from being in very close touch with her daughter. As it was, the first ten or twelve years of V S-W's life do not seem to have been remarkable for the close contact between mother and daughter. According to V S-W:

she loved me when I was a baby, but I don't think she cared much for me as a child, nor do I blame her. My principal recollection of her then is that I used to be taken to her room to be 'passed' before going down to luncheon on party days, when I had had my hair crimped; and I was always wrong and miserable[20]

and again:

I can't remember much about my childhood, except that I had very long legs and very straight hair, over which Mother used to hurt my feelings and say she could not bear to look at me because I was so ugly;[21]

V S-W was an only child, and Lady Sackville seems to have made no secret of the fact that she would never have any brothers or sisters, for V S-W notes that "she says she would have drowned herself sooner than have another child".[22]

Frequently V S-W had to spend considerable periods alone at Knole with her grandfather when her parents were away on visits. Old Lord Sackville, who was then nearly eighty, was strange company for a young and sensitive girl. He was eccentric and morose, although he liked children and had many little private jokes with V S-W. Her recollection of him was as being:

very old, and queer, and silent. He hated people, and never spoke to the people who came to the house; in fact, if he got the chance he used to go to London for the day when he knew people were coming, and I used to be left alone to entertain them.[23]

and further:

Of all human beings, he was surely the most inscrutable. I lived with him for sixteen years, and had I lived with him for yet another sixteen I have no doubt that he would have remained just as much of an enigma.[24]

[18] See *The Times*, 8 August 1913, p. 11.
[19] *Pepita*, pp. 242—6. The case "Capron v. Scott" was reported very fully in *The Times*, 17 June, 1913, p. 3; 25 June pp. 5, 8; 27 June, p. 67; 28 June, p. 5; 1 July, p. 5; 2 July, p. 5; 4 July, p. 5; 5 July, p. 5; 8 July, p. 5.
[20] MS Autobiography, p. 12. For details of this work, see p. 109, note 1.
[21] *Ibid.*, p. 2.
[22] *Ibid.*, p. 12.
[23] *Ibid.*, p. 3.
[24] *Ibid.*, p. 6.

Apart from her hours in the schoolroom and her social duties, few restrictions were placed on V S-W; her time was very much her own to do what she liked with. She describes herself in 1900 as:

> always grubby and in tatters; my dogs, absorbingly adored; my rabbits, who used to 'course' in secret with my dogs, and whose offspring I used to throw over the garden wall when they became too numerous; the trenches I dug in the garden during the war; the 'army' I raised and commanded amongst the terrorised children of the neighbourhood; my khaki suit, and the tears of rage I shed because I was not allowed to have it made with trousers,—no, nor so much as a proper kilt; ... [I] see myself, plain, lean, dark, unsociable, unattractive,—horribly unattractive! rough, and secret. Secrecy was my passion; I daresay that was why I hated companions.[25]

It is clear that V S-W considered herself a disappointment to her mother, who openly reproached her with a lack of attractiveness and social grace, for nowhere has she ever recorded that her mother complimented her on her appearance or gave her any encouragement.

It is therefore interesting to see what references to her daughter Lady Sackville made in her diary. Personal comments are relatively few, considering that she was a regular and fairly voluminous diarist; up to 1904, when V S-W was twelve, most of the entries concerning her deal with colds and other childish complaints. There are, however, several references to V S-W's appearance, such as:

> The drawing of Vita's by Mr Stock is finished and is quite pretty, but the child is much prettier and has far more depth and animation in her face. I took her to Mrs Freddy Bentinck's fancy-dress ball in her old fancy dress and powdered hair: she was lovely.[26]

Lady Sackville's appreciation of her daughter's appearance was, however, apparently subjective: comments on her good looks may have been seen as a compliment to herself, and when she writes "Vita and I went to lunch at the Marlboroughs' at Blenheim. Vita was looking so pretty and was much admired",[27] she quite possibly meant that she herself was flattered to have a daughter about whom people said nice things to her. Judging from V S-W's Autobiography previously quoted, she does not seem to have passed the compliments on to her daughter.

V S-W must have felt that she was a disappointment to her father, too, although, unlike her mother, he never seems to have indicated in any way that this was so. She must have realized that he needed an heir to whom he could hand over Knole:

> Such a man, of course, ought to have had a smoothly running home; lots of children; sons whom he could teach to shoot and fish and ride and accept responsibility against the day when it should be theirs[28]

Further confirmation of her feeling is to be found in Mr Nigel Nicolson's introduction to his father's diaries,[29] and in a letter V S-W wrote to Harold Nicolson in 1950 (quoted on p. 26 infra).[30]

It is not surprising, therefore, in view of her mother's disparagement and her own sense of having failed her parents in some way, that V S-W suffered from a marked sense of inferiority which found expression in an attitude of defiance and pretended

[25] *Ibid.*, p. 10.
[26] Lady Sackville's Diary, 20 February, 1903.
[27] *Ibid.*, 17 August, 1906.
[28] *Pepita*, pp. 237—8.
[29] *Diaries and Letters, 1930—39*, p. 17.
[30] *Diaries and Letters, 1945—62*, p. 195.

indifference to the opinions of others. This is clearly indicated in the following description she gave of herself:

I think that between the ages of thirteen and nineteen I must have been quite dreadful. I was plain, priggish, studious, (oh, very!) totally uninspired, unmanageably and lankily tall, in fact the only good thing that could be said of me was that I wouldn't have anything to do with my kind. Seeing that I was unpopular, (small wonder, for a saturnine prig,) I wouldn't court popularity. I minded rather, and used to cry when I went to bed after coming home from a party, but I made myself defiant about it. I don't mean this to sound in the least pathetic; I wasn't unhappy, only solitary, but I don't pretend that I minded solitude, I rather chose it.[31]

This defiance was also manifest in her attitude to school. Her early education had been at home, in the hands of a governess, but when she reached her teens, she was sent to Miss Woolf's school in London as a day-pupil. She makes no bones about her urge to compensate herself for her weaknesses:

I set myself to triumph at that school, and I did triumph,—I beat everybody there, sooner or later, and at the end-of-term exams I thought I had done badly if I didn't carry off at least six out of eight first prizes. I think I was quite self-conscious over this: if I couldn't be popular, I would be clever.[32]

Nevertheless, the nagging doubt has not been banished, for she continues with assumed bravado:

I wasn't hated at that school, at least I don't think so; I think they quite liked me. But I really cared not a scrap whether they liked me or not; those were my most savage years![33]

As V S-W grew older, the relationship between her parents deteriorated steadily. Their position was not always an easy one while old Lord Sackville was alive, for V S-W's father, although the heir, was not the son. After his death in 1908 it was rendered still more difficult by the lawsuit to decide the succession to the title, and, to an even greater degree, by the rather straitened financial circumstances in which they found themselves after paying death duties. This was not made easier to bear by Lady Sackville's utter lack of any sense of the value of money; quite capable of spending two thousand pounds on a diamond necklace on the spur of the moment,[34] she was also capable of the most incredible economies the next moment. Thus she would buy notepaper from the most expensive stationer in London, but she seldom wrote her letters on anything but old scraps of paper that she did not like to throw away. One of her most satisfactory discoveries was that the toilet paper in the Ladies Cloakroom at Harrods made quite excellent notepaper, and she wrote on it to V S-W, "*Regarde, comme ce papier prend beaucoup mieux l'encre que le Bromo.*"[35]

The increasing strain between V S-W's parents led to ugly little scenes sometimes and brought out the ruthlessness in Lady Sackville of which V S-W was afraid. She writes:

I remember very vividly terrible scenes between her and Dada,—at least, she made the scene, he usually said nothing at all, or very mildly: 'Oh, come, dear, is that quite accurate?'[36]

and again:

---

[31] MS Autobiography, pp. 17—8.
[32] *Ibid.*, p. 18.
[33] *Ibid.*, p. 19.
[34] *Pepita*, p. 246.
[35] *Ibid.*, p. 206.
[36] MS Autobiography, p. 3.

21

There certainly *was* something ruthless about Mother, and one of the things that has left the strongest and cruellest impression upon me was a horrible little dialogue I overheard once in London, as I lay in bed in the dark next door; she was alone with Grandpapa, and was evidently very much annoyed over something, for I heard her telling him how much in the way he was, with that sort of *flick* in her voice that to this day makes me shudder; and he was moved to protest,—he, who never said a word! . . . I wish I could forget that little dialogue, but I can't; it burnt.[37]

Up to the time of her marriage, V S-W must, in some respects, have been rather immature. Certainly as far as her mother was concerned, she seems to have been unable to adopt an independent outlook, and it was many years before she was able to look at her objectively and see her character as it really was.

In later life V S-W realised this herself, as she shows in her MS Autobiography, written in 1920, where she says that she had really only grasped that few of her mother's statements were accurate a comparatively short time before.[38] The reason why she failed to realise this earlier, at an age when most young people have begun to understand the motives which drive their parents to act in the way they do, must have been that she was afraid of her mother's temper and was so completely dominated by her immensely strong personality.[39] A clear indication of this can be seen in an entry in Lady Sackville's diary for 1910. The occasion was an amateur theatrical performance, in which V S-W had taken part, followed by a dinner-party at their home.

I wanted to take Vita home, but she objected to come and got Lionel to support her and openly disobeyed me. I am extremely angry with L and V, with L for making V disobey my authority, as she ought to have changed at once and helped me preparing for the invasion that followed . . . Lionel came to speak to me and apologised for having interfered between Vita and me. Nothing could have been nicer than the gentle way in which he spoke—so I forgave him, but I stipulated very clearly that I wish to have full authority on Vita as I sh[d] never make her do anything wrong against him. Vita came up to my room after dinner and sobbed till 12 o'cl, poor child.[40]

V S-W was eighteen and a half years old at the time.

Although V S-W must subconsciously have hated her mother as well as loved her, she was no more proof against her overwhelming charm than any of the other people who met her. She was constantly being humiliated and trodden down, which, to a sensitive child, must have been agony, but at the same time she admired and adored her mother. She shows the ambivalence of her feelings when she writes:

How my mother puzzled me, and how I loved her! She wounded and dazzled and fascinated and charmed me by turns. Sometimes she was downright unjust, and accused me of things I had never done, lies I had never told, . . . but how she could always win me round, however unjust she had been, just by looking at me and saying: 'Perhaps we have had a little misunderstanding.' . . . she had been really unjust, accusing me of telling a lie which I happened not to have told; children are sensitive about such things, and at the bottom of their hearts they know the difference between truth and untruth; on this occasion I knew that I had

[37] *Ibid.*, p. 5.
[38] *Ibid.*, p. 3.
[39] Eloquent testimony to the strength of her personality was given by the celebrated F. E. Smith, during the law suit over Sir John's will: "He asked the jury whether, in all their acquaintance with the courts, they ever saw a lady of a more arresting and dominating personality . . . than Lady Sackville? The jury had seen in the witness-box one of the strongest and most striking personalities they had met in their lives." *Daily Chronicle*, 8 July, 1913, p. 5.
[40] Lady Sackville's Diary, 2 June, 1910.

told the truth, but my mother made me kneel at her feet, which humiliated me and hurt my pride, and said that I must ask God to forgive me[41]

Lady Sackville always seems to have had this twofold power over V S-W; at one moment making her suffer, either by humiliating her, wounding her deepest feelings, crushing her or even by rendering her acutely embarrassed; and at the next, inspiring in her a devotion that was doubly strong for having been preceded by the diametrically opposite emotion:

Of course she always put me to acute embarrassment by the unconventionality of her behaviour wherever she was; thus she always remained convinced that no one understood French except herself and me, and would make personal remarks at the top of her voice in that language. 'Mais regarde donc cette vieille horreur, ma chérie: qu'est ce qu'elle a l'air, avec cette perruque-là? Peut-on s'affubler ainsi!' It was quite in vain that I tried to stem the flow of such comments whenever we went to a shop or to a matinée together ... Oh yes, she was fun, she was enchanting, she was embarrassing, she made me feel hot with shame,—and then, seeing her visibly charm the tired shop-assistant behind the counter, or watching her lovely profile beside me in the darkened theatre as she fanned herself with that unmistakably Spanish gesture, ... I would have died for her, I would have murdered anyone that breathed a word against her, I would have suffered any injustice at her hands.[42]

This ambivalence in V S-W's attitude to her mother must have played an important part in the development of her character. For many years she was haunted by her inability to come to terms with her conflicting feelings about her mother, and this conflict is, as we shall see, reflected in some of her writing during this time;[43] in her books, particularly the novels, the figure of Lady Sackville appears at times in some guise or other, either good or bad. It was not until after Lady Sackville's death in 1936 that V S-W seems to have been able to write her out of her system with any degree of success. Pepita, written in 1937, tells the story of V S-W's Spanish grandmother and her family; in actual fact it would seem to be her own mother, Pepita's daughter, that V S-W is analysing and trying to explain to herself in this book. After this date her mother figures very little in her works.

V S-W's childhood was, in many respects, an unsatisfying, even an unhappy one. An only child, much left alone with her old and queer grandfather as her only true companion, lacking intimate contact with the mother she adored and hated or with the father she loved and admired, and suffering from a strong feeling of inferiority, she was thrown back almost entirely on her own resources. She was singularly isolated and lacking in confidants. As she was educated at home until she reached her teens, she had no school friends and, apart from her grandfather, there was almost no one with whom she could associate on an equal footing. She was surrounded by servants, many of whom she knew well and had had around her all her life, but, as she says, "My child, remember who you *are*" was a phrase frequently to be heard proceeding from the lips of governess or chaperone.[44] She played with the local children from Sevenoaks, but it is clear that she did not play with them as equals; to them she must always have been the lady from the great house, and she tyrannised over them, ordering them about with hereditary authority:

[41] *Pepita,* p. 206.
[42] *Ibid.,* pp. 232—3.
[43] See infra, p. 28, for an example.
[44] *Pepita,* p. 181.

I know I was cruel to other children, because I remember stuffing their nostrils with putty and beating a little boy with stinging nettles, and I lost nearly all my friends in that kind of way, until none of the local children would come to tea with me except those who had acted as my allies and lieutenants.[45]

There were children's parties with her equals too; many of them, for V S-W's diary contains numerous references to the parties she has been to, but they were under the eyes of mothers, her own included, and her feeling of inferiority would probably have prevented her from being herself. She cannot have enjoyed these parties.[46]

Then there were the frequent house-parties and entertainments given by Lady Sackville at Knole. V S-W was expected to attend these, but what she saw there was to inspire her with a revulsion for Society that was to remain with her to the end of her life. This is apparent in several of her books, as we shall see, but perhaps it is most clearly expressed in *The Edwardians*:

> Leonard Antequil, watching them from outside, marvelled to see them so easily pleased. Here are a score of people, he thought, who by virtue of their position are accustomed to the intimate society of princes, politicians, financiers, wits, beauties, and other makers of history, yet are apparently content with desultory chatter and make-believe occupation throughout the long hours of an idle day. . . . He listened carefully, tabulating their topics. They were more interested, he observed, in facts than ideas. A large proportion of their conversation seemed to consist in asking one another what they had thought of such-and-such an entertainment, and whether they were going to such-and-such an other, . . . These parties of theirs, he thought, were like chain-smoking: each cigarette was lighted in the hope that it might be more satisfying than the last. Then investments bulked heavy in their talk, and other people's incomes, and the merits of various stocks and shares; . . . If this is Society, thought Antequil, God help us, for surely no fraud has ever equalled it. These are the people, or a sample of them, who ordain the London season, glorify Ascot, make or unmake the fortune of small Continental watering-places, inspire envy, emulation, and snobbishness—well, thought Antequil, with a shrug, they spend money, and that is the best that can be said for them.[47]

The first chapter of *The Edwardians* seems, in fact, to be an accurate description of the life that V S-W must have led as a child. Sebastian and Viola, who in this chapter may well represent the male and female aspects of V S-W's personality, suffer as she suffered from a mother's dominating character, feel the same lack of self-confidence, share the same love of Chevron/Knole.

Although V S-W's childhood can hardly have been a happy one, there was compensation, and there was escape—not physical escape, although she mentions quite casually that "I forgot to say that two or three times I tried to run away, but was always brought back".[48] It was, perhaps, just because of her isolation that compensation and escape come to be of such importance to her.

The compensation was first and foremost Knole; the escape was writing.

The importance which Knole had both for V S-W's writing[49] and for the development of her personality can scarcely be overstated. From her earliest childhood she had wandered about the great house until she knew intimately every one of its three hundred

[45] MS Autobiography, p. 3.
[46] *Ibid.*, p. 18.
[47] *The Edwardians*, pp. 12—5. See also infra, p. 58. Note that in this dissertation, the edition of *The Edwardians* used is that published by Arrow Books Ltd., London, 1960.
[48] MS Autobiography, p. 10.
[49] See infra, p. 37.

and sixty-five rooms, its galleries, its fifty-two staircases, its seven courtyards. After being in the hands of the Sackville family for almost four hundred years, the whole house was filled with family history, and during her early life V S-W became imbued with a deep sense of family tradition. Several factors probably contributed to strengthen even further the bonds between her and Knole. Her isolation from people, her hatred of companions, "a trait I inherit from my family",[50] her lack of true contact with her mother, her awareness of the rootless Spanish-gipsy strain in her;[51] all these may have tended to make her seek identification with Knole as a symbol of permanance, as firm ground beneath her feet. She turned to Knole for companionship and endowed the house with a living personality:

> Knole is not haunted, but you require either an unimaginative nerve or else a complete certainty of the house's benevolence before you can wander through the state-rooms after nightfall with a candle, as I used to do when I was little. . . . But I was never frightened at Knole. I loved it; and took it for granted that Knole loved me.[52]

It was to Knole that V S-W transferred the love that in other children is normally lavished on people. This feeling for Knole was so powerful that places came to usurp the position of people in her scale of values, as she herself admits when, many years later, she wrote in a letter to Harold Nicolson:

> You know me well enough to know that people don't count very much with me. I love places (Sissinghurst, the Dordogne, Florence) far more than I care for people, and Rollo [her Alsatian dog] probably means more to me than any of my friends. And of course Knole . . . but that is a separate thing I can't speak about. That goes too deep.[53]

This should not be taken to mean that she had no interest in people; she had. But she found personal relations with people so difficult that she much preferred meeting strangers to her friends, and felt more at home with her dog and in places which she found congenial than in the company of people. As she once let slip in 1945 in a letter to Harold Nicolson, "How much I prefer strangers to my friends."[54] The feeling of her inability to establish contact with other people haunted her all her life. It is the theme of an undated poem that she probably wrote about 1940:

> There are times when I cannot endure the sight of people.
> I know they are charming, intelligent, since everybody tells me so,
> But I wish they would go away.
> I cannot establish contact with anybody;
> They are all unreal to me, the charming intelligent people,
> And I daresay I seem as unreal to them.
> Yet I am real to myself,—or am I not?
> Anyhow I delude myself into some sort of reality,
> But when they come, the charming intelligent people,
> I lose all illusion of reality, whether my own or theirs.[55]

[50] MS Autobiography, p. 10.
[51] See infra, pp. 33—4.
[52] Knole and the Sackvilles, pp. 28—9.
[53] Diaries and Letters, 1945—62, p. 322.
[54] Diaries and Letters, 1939—45, p. 472.
[55] MS in the possession of Mr Nigel Nicolson, Sissinghurst Castle. See also the poem "I suppose other people endure the same dissatisfactions", on p. 117 infra.

The depth of her feelings for Knole was probably unknown even to herself until she finally had to abandon all hope of ever owning it. As Knole was entailed, she must have grown up with the conscious knowledge that it could never be hers, that it must eventually pass to her uncle, Charles Sackville-West, and thence to his son, Edward, born in 1901. In 1903, when V S-W was not quite eleven years old, the idea seems already to be firmly planted in her mind, for Lady Sackville records in her diary:

Took Vita with me to spend the day with Charles[56] and be introduced to Eddie[57] . . . and Vita was very nice to him in spite of her jealousy of him.[58]

But however much one may understand the inevitable with one's mind, one is nevertheless quite unprepared for the strength of one's reactions when the event actually happens. In V S-W's case there was also the story of how Pepita's illegitimate daughter had become chatelaine at Knole to show her that the unexpected can happen. When, therefore, her father died in 1928 and Knole passed to her Uncle Charles, the blow was no less for being expected. Her love of Knole was so deep and so integral a part of her being that she never really recoverd from the loss, and even in 1950, twenty-two years later, she could write to Harold Nicolson:

Oh Hadji [her name for Harold Nicolson], my Knole, my Knole! I have just been writing to Uncle Charlie [Lord Sackville] to ask him if he could supply me with a key to the garden-gate. I always had a master-key, but it got lost during the sale at Long Barn. It isn't that I would ever want to use it; it is only that I would like to have it by me, in case on some summer evening I wanted to go there, as I have often been tempted to do, letting myself into the garden secretly, and I couldn't bear the idea of being locked out. Oh God, I do wish that Knole hadn't got such a hold on my heart! If only I had been Dada's son, instead of his daughter! I hoped that I had damped down the fire into embers, but the embers blow up into a flame at one breath, so easily.[59]

Although she had the key of Knole, she could not bring herself to use it until 1961, one year before her death.[60]

V S-W's awareness of her feelings about Knole must have been greatly sharpened by the law-suit to decide the inheritance of the title in 1910, when she was 18 years old, for upon the outcome of the case depended whether she would continue to live at the house or not. The relief and feeling of security engendered by the fact that her parents won the case would have made the ultimate loss of Knole an even greater tragedy for her, for who is proof against the conviction that a miracle may again happen? The fact remains that, when Knole passed to her uncle in 1928, something happened to V S-W that was to leave its mark on everything she wrote and thought.

According to V S-W herself, she began to write in about 1904:

When I was about twelve I started to write, (it was Cyrano de Bergerac that first initiated me to the possibilities of literature!) and I never stopped writing after that,—historical novels, pretentious, quite uninteresting, pedantic, and all written at unflagging speed: the day after one was finished another would be begun.[61]

In fact, her memory seems to be at fault here, for her first novel, about Edward Sack-

---

[56] V S-W's uncle, Charles Sackville-West, later 4th Baron Sackville.
[57] V S-W's cousin, Edward Sackville-West, later 5th Baron Sackville.
[58] Entry for 25th February, 1903.
[59] *Diaries and Letters, 1945—62*, p. 196.
[60] *Ibid.*, pp. 397, 443.
[61] MS Autobiography, p. 17.

ville,[62] is dated 1906, when she would have been thirteen or fourteen. She wrote it, as she did the following works, straight into a thick folio volume; they are remarkable for the almost complete absence of alteration and addition.

The following year saw the completion of two plays in French, "Le Masque de Fer" and "Jean-Baptiste Poquelin" and a novel in English, "The King's Secret".[63] More important to her, perhaps, was the fact that she entered the *Onlooker* verse competition and won a prize. She comments:

> £1. I had won in the Onlooker verse competition. This is the first money I have got through working. I hope (as I am to restore the fortunes of the family) that it will not be the last.[64]

It is rather touching to find out that the competition consisted of supplying the last line to a limerick, and that V S-W was one of five winners.

In later life V S-W was extremely secretive about what she was writing; her husband and children used to say that "we only really knew what she was thinking when we opened her latest novel."[65] In those days, however, she used to show her books to her mother in manuscript. Lady Sackville writes:

> I have finished reading her book on Charles II, The King's Secret. It really is very good, if not a little too long in the dialogues. But the character of the boy Cranfield is well delineated. She meant him to be her own self that she portrayed! And he is a dear, lovable child.[66]

It is clear, however, that whatever she may have felt about her daughter's writing, Lady Sackville must have belittled its value to V S-W, discouraging her with faint praise and the cold voice of parental common sense. In *Chatterton,* the verse drama V S-W had privately printed in 1909, the following dialogue occurs when Chatterton, full of dreams about his future as a poet, comes home after winning a prize at school for the poem he has written:

Mistress Chatterton.
>These little follies and these little whims,
>They mean so much to thee just now, dear son,
>But in a few years' time thou wilt forget
>That ever thou did'st love to sit and dream,
>And that thy verse was as a god to thee.

Chatterton.
>So truly, mother, youth's ambitions fade
>And pass away?

Mistress Chatterton.
>They do, and thou, poor child,
>Wilt soon be smiling at the tragedies
>That seem so serious and fill thy life.

Chatterton.
>And am I but a child?

Mistress Chatterton.
>At seventeen?
>What else? A foolish child![67]

---

[62] "Edward Sackville, Earl of Dorset."
[63] The MSS of all these plays and novels are at Sissinghurst Castle.
[64] V S-W's diary, 12th July, 1907.
[65] *Diaries and Letters, 1930—39,* p. 16.
[66] Lady Sackville's diary, 16th October, 1907.
[67] *Chatterton* I:4.

The main themes of *Chatterton* are two: first, the poet's uncertainty as to the value of his inspiration and writing. The stimulance he feels when his friend Archer reassures him of his genius and encourages him to break away from his home in order to devote himself to the great work he has to do. Then comes the reverse. The effect of Walpole's condemnation of Chatterton's writing as a worthless forgery is to make him so downcast and convinced of his failure as a poet that he destroys his own works before committing suicide. Chatterton, in the play, appears to suffer from the same doubts, fears and reactions to positive or adverse criticism as did V S-W herself. The second theme, the nature and origin of inspiration itself, was a subject about which V S-W felt less doubt:

> *Archer.*
> And thou? know'st thou what inspiration means?
> *Chatterton.*
> Do I? Who can tell? At any rate,
> I know what it may mean to leave the earth
> In spirit, while the body, dead machine,
> Unconsciously records the spirit's thoughts.
> My eyes, my hands, are strangers to me then,
> I scarcely know what they will make me do.
> I am not present, and my will is gone;
> Some other will compels me to obey,
> And sways me,—hell or heaven-born, who knows?[68]

It is also significant that Chatterton considers himself and the importance of the work he is doing greatly misunderstood by his mother:

> *Chatterton.*
> I love thee, mother, but thou pain'st me so!
> Thou dost not understand me; it is sad
> When those we love most, understand us least.[69]

In these early years V S-W spent some time away from Knole travelling in various parts of Europe. After Sir John Murray Scott had become a friend of the family in about 1900, it was the custom for them all to go to Paris and live in his apartment for some time every summer.[70] In the autumn, the whole party would move up to Scotland for the shooting and fishing—Sir John was a keen sportsman despite his 25 stone. These summers in Paris meant a great deal to V S-W, who was acutely conscious of the grace and beauty of Sir John's apartment and Bagatelle.[71]

From 1908 onwards V S-W, and sometimes her mother, took to spending springtime in Italy; the first year in Pisa and Milan, later in Florence, for which V S-W developed a great love. In the autumn of 1909, Sir John and Lady Sackville took V S-W with them on a tour of Russia, Poland and Austria. Russia in particular made a deep impression on V S-W, who wrote on their return, "How much I loved Russia! those vast fields, that feudal life, that illimitable horizon,—oh how shall I ever be able to live in this restricted island?"[72]

1910 was the year that V S-W "came out", a process that she found exceedingly

[68] *Ibid.,* I:6.
[69] *Ibid.,* I:5.
[70] *Pepita,* pp. 197—8.
[71] *Ibid.,* pp. 193—8.
[72] MS Autobiography, p. 24.

disagreeable; fortunately for her, the death of King Edward VII saved her from a great many festivities. However, at one small dinner party she met Harold Nicolson. She was eighteen; he was twenty-three, a young diplomatist:

> The first remark I ever heard him make was 'What fun!' when he was asked by his hostess to act as host. Everything was fun to his energy, vitality, and buoyancy. I liked his irrepressible brown curls, his laughing eyes, his charming smile, and his boyishness.[73]

That summer V S-W was seriously ill with pneumonia. Lady Sackville rented a villa just outside Monte Carlo to which she took her daughter to spend the whole winter so that she should have every chance of recuperating quickly. Harold Nicolson (subsequently referred to as H.N.) was a frequent visitor when he was able to get away from Madrid, where he had been posted. After the usual spring visit to Italy, V S-W and her mother returned to Knole, where they spent the rest of the year.[74]

In January 1912, Sir John died suddenly. A few days later H.N. proposed to V S-W.[75] It was not, perhaps, the moment he would have chosen for the occasion, but he was to go to Constantinople at the end of the month and he wished to know where he stood before leaving. V S-W accepted him, but as Lady Sackville did not think H.N. an entirely satisfactory suitor for her daughter, who she considered would be marrying beneath her in accepting a man who would not be in a position to keep her as she was used to being kept, she refused to allow the engagement to be made public.[75]

H.N. returned from Constantinople in August 1912. The moment was still not propitious for the announcement of their engagement, for Sir John's will was not yet proved, and it was known that his family were furious about the legacy to Lady Sackville and intended to contest it. However, H.N. and V S-W were able to spend the better part of two months together at Knole, after which they and Rosamund Grosvenor, a friend of hers, spent the following six months in Italy. When H.N. had to return to Constantinople in the spring, V S-W and Rosamund Grosvenor went on to Spain together.[76]

The lawsuit about Sir John's will came to court in June 1913. When Lady Sackville had won her case, she gave V S-W and H.N. permission to announce their engagement and arrange the wedding for the autumn. On 1st October, 1913, they were married in the private chapel at Knole. V S-W writes:

> Mother, who doesn't like being émotionée, stayed in bed.[77]

[73] *Ibid.*, p. 24.
[74] *Ibid.*, p. 25.
[75] *Ibid.*, p. 29.
[76] *Ibid.*, p. 31.
[77] *Ibid.*, p. 34.

The Years 1913 to 1929

Harold Nicolson was born in Teheran in 1886, the third son of Sir Arthur Nicolson (later Lord Carnock), a diplomatist of Scottish family, and Catherine Rowan Hamilton, a younger sister of Lady Dufferin. His boyhood and youth were spent in the legations and embassies at which his father was stationed, in Constantinople, Sophia, Tangier, Madrid and St. Petersburg, or at the Ulster houses of his mother's family. When he began school, he was sent first to a private school at Folkestone, and then on to Wellington College and Balliol. In 1909 he passed into the Foreign Office, having come second in the entrance examination, one of the most competitive of the day.[1] The following year he met V S-W.

By temperament H.N. was entirely different from V S-W. He was gay, boyish, generous; the sort of man that people take an instant liking to. But at the same time he was an intellectual aristocrat, acutely conscious of the fact that he belonged to an élite of intelligence and achievement. He could be lacking in charity to those whom he felt to be his mental inferiors, and all his life he was prejudiced against most Americans, Jews, all coloured and Levantine peoples, and most of the middle and working classes; failings of which he was aware.[2] To those with whom he felt an affinity, however, he was a delightful companion, being by nature a good conversationalist and a person who loved good company.[3]

The marriage between H.N. and V S-W was, despite the great differences in their characters and temperaments, an extremely successful one, although not without its perilous moments. It was, to use a hackneyed expression which here happens to suit perfectly, a true marriage of minds, for what, above all, attracted each of them was the intellectual quality of the other's mind.

V S-W regarded "Harold far more as a playfellow than in any other light. Our relationship was so fresh, so intellectual, so *un*physical, that I never thought of him in that aspect at all."[4]

Even during their engagement this side of their relationship had been dominant in her mind:

> He was as gay and clever as ever, and I loved his brain and his youth, . . . I did like him better than anyone, as a companion and playfellow, and for his brain and his delicious disposition.[5]

[1] See *Diaries and Letters, 1930—39*, p. 23.
[2] *Ibid.*, pp. 24—5, 189—90.
[3] *Ibid.*, p. 25.
[4] MS Autobiography, p. 30.
[5] *Ibid.*, p. 27.

A few days after the wedding H.N. and V S-W left England to spend their honeymoon in Italy and Egypt before going on to Constantinople, where H.N. had to resume his duties at the Embassy. Six months later, with the threat of war growing ever closer, H.N. was recalled to England, where they arrived in June 1914. Shortly afterwards, their first son, Benedict, was born. V S-W writes:

I remember a divine voyage by sea from Constantinople to Marseilles, through the Aegean, a second honeymoon. We met Mother in Paris, and both thought that she was going off her head, as she was obviously in an extraordinarily unbalanced state of mind. Then we went to Knole. War was declared on the 4th of August, and Ben was born on the 6th. Scenes immediately began with Mother over his name, and they culminated in our taking a house in London as it was impossible for us to remain with Mother. We spent the winter in London, and I became quite sociable.[6]

The house they bought was 182 Ebury Street, in Pimlico—the house that Mozart had lived in when he was in London. It had belonged to Lady Sackville, who had had it largely rebuilt with the help of Sir Edwin Lutyens a few years before.[7] However, even if V S-W felt that she could never again live at Knole for fear of further disagreements with her mother, it seemed that neither could she bear to be out of reach of it, for in the summer of 1915 she and H.N. bought Long Barn, a 16th century house only two miles away from her beloved Knole.[8] Here, in Kent, they used to spend every summer until 1925, when H.N. was posted to Teheran as Counsellor, when they sold the house in Ebury Street and moved to Long Barn permanently. In 1917 her second son, Nigel, was born in London.

These war-time years were probably the most contented of her life. She was able to see every day the husband she adored and there were only her children to distract her attention from him alone. Apart from the disagreements with her mother, she seems to have had no worries. She was writing poetry. When, in 1920, she looked back on these years, she said:

That was the only period of my life when I achieved anything like popularity: I was no longer plain, I took adequate trouble to make myself agreeable, Harold was loved by everyone who met him, we were, in fact, a nice young couple to ask out to dinner. Oh God, the horror of it! I was so happy that I forgot even to suffer from Wanderlust.[9]

In 1917 V S-W achieved true publication when John Lane accepted her *Poems of West and East*.[10] The themes of some of the poems in this volume are themes that are to recur time and again in her poetry, but here, in this first book, they are strangely muted and without the passion with which they are later to be stated. "To Knole, October 1, 1913" is a leave-taking of the house on the day of her marriage, but the note of anguish with which she was later to refer to Knole is not present. Only two of the poems, "Disillusion" and "Resolution", contain signs of the intensely personal self-examination and reflection which were to be characteristic of much of V S-W's poetry.

After the end of the war, H.N. was sent to Paris as one of the members of the British Delegation to the Paris Peace Conference. For the services he rendered there he was awarded the C.M.G. at the early age of 34.[11] However, his enforced absence from

[6] *Ibid.*, p. 36.
[7] Letter dated 23/11/70 from Mr Nigel Nicolson to the present author.
[8] Letter dated 1/1/71 from Mr Nigel Nicolson to the present author.
[9] MS Autobiography, p. 36.
[10] Of the twenty-two poems in this volume, one, "The Dancing Elf", had been published in the *English Review* in August 1913, and eight poems published privately in *Constantinople*, 1915.
[11] *Diaries and Letters, 1930—39*, p. 29.

home and his family for considerable periods, the first since their marriage five years before, led, directly or indirectly, to a grave crisis in his relationship with V S-W.

In a work such as this, family relationships can only be relevant insofar as they affect the writing and personality of the subject of the study. Before deciding whether the nature of this crisis needs to be discussed, it is therefore necessary to consider whether it is of importance to a full understanding of the author's works. As the answer in this case must be an uncompromising "yes", it will be of interest to see what indications available printed sources have to offer about the causes of this crisis.

Writing more than thirty-five years later, V S-W said in a letter to H.N.:

> I thought the other day, in the night, that you were the only person I have ever really loved. I thought this out rather carefully, and analysed my feelings, and came to that conclusion. I won't say that I haven't been *in love* with other people, but you are the only person that I have ever deeply and painfully loved. That is true.[12]

Further illumination is provided by H.N., who wrote in his diary in December 1933:

> Viti is not a person one can take for granted. She is a dark river moving deeply in shadows. She really does not care for the domestic affections. She would wish life to be conducted on a series of *grandes passions*. Or she thinks she would. In practice, had I been a passionate man, I should have suffered tortures of jealousy on her behalf, have made endless scenes, and we should now be separated, I living in Montevideo as H.M. Minister and she breeding Samoyeds in the Gobi desert.[13]

This extract, which, as it stands, is liable to misinterpretation, is put into its right perspective by two remarks made by Nigel Nicolson. He says firstly:

> My brother and I understood her better than we would reveal. We understood her masculinity, her enduring regret that she was not born a boy . . .[14]

and, secondly:

> The interplay of male and female characteristics in each of them [V S-W and H.N.], and in their relationship with each other, is the most absorbing aspect of their marriage.[15]

Taken together, these extracts would seem to indicate that V S-W was attracted to her own sex. If one turns to her works to obtain confirmation of this, one is soon struck by phrases such as "one wonders how they had ever brought themselves to commit the grotesque act necessary to beget children";[16] by the comparison in *The Dark Island* between the feelings engendered in Shirin by the advances made towards her by men, and those she receives from Cristina;[17] by the relationship that appears to exist between Evelyn and Ruth in *Family History;*[18] by the poems contained in *King's Daughter.*[19] The cumulative effect of all this makes it reasonable to assume that this crisis in V S-W and H.N.'s marriage was because of a liason between her and another woman. That their marriage was able to survive the strain was mainly due to the fact that the very real and deep love that they felt for each other sprang from intellectual rather than physical roots. Having survived, it could deepen into what Nigel Nicolson has called "one of the strangest and most successful unions that two gifted people have ever enjoyed."[20]

[12] *Diaries and Letters, 1945—62*, p. 322.
[13] *Diaries and Letters, 1930—39*, p. 158.
[14] *Ibid.*, p. 17.
[15] *Diaries and Letters, 1945—62*, p. 22.
[16] *Grand Canyon*, Michael Joseph, London, 1942, p. 19.
[17] Hogarth Press, London, 1934, pp. 44, 175, 177, 259—60.
[18] Hogarth Press, London, 1932, pp. 44—5, 49—50, 81, 293—4.
[19] Hogarth Press, London, 1929.
[20] *Diaries and Letters, 1930—39*, p. 22.

Closely connected with this trait in V S-W's nature, or perhaps one form of expression that it took, was the dual personality that she suffered from most of her life. Basically it must have arisen out of her intense regret that she had not been born a boy, but it was probably complicated by her acute awareness of the gipsy blood in her. She was afraid of it; afraid it would appear in her as she thought it had in Lady Sackville, of whom she said, "it accounts for much of Mother, who at times is pure, undiluted peasant."[21]

The conception of heredity played an important part in her early works, particularly those in prose; indeed, her first novel, published in 1919, was entitled simply *Heritage*. On the face of it, this is just a love story, but closer examination reveals that it is also something else. The background of the story is V S-W's own ancestry—Captain Pennistan from the Weald of Kent had met and fallen in love with a beautiful Spanish dancer, and had brought her home as his bride. But the story itself is not concerned directly with them. It is about the two grand-daughters of the marriage, Nancy, whose appearance is purely English but whose temperament is Spanish, her sister Ruth, whose appearance is Spanish but who has inherited little of her grandmother's fire, and about Rawdon Westmacott, her cousin, who has both her appearance and her temperament.

To him Ruth is irresistibly drawn, despite the fact she hates him.

V S-W's conception of heredity in this book has been strongly influenced by Francis Galton's experimental mating of a common brown mouse with a dancing mouse. She mentions the experiment and describes how "in the subsequent generations the common brown house mouse predominated, but every now and then there came a mouse that waltzed and waltzed, restless and tormented, until in the endless pursuit of its tail it died, dazed, blinded, perplexed, by the relentless fate that had it in its grip."[22]

The central theme of the story is really the mutual attraction and repulsion felt by Ruth and Rawdon—two facets of V S-W's character. Ruth says, "He cringes to me, and then I bully him; or else he bullies me, and then I cringe to him. But quarrel as we may, we always come together again."[23]

The narrator, who is also deeply involved emotionally, comments:

"Ruth loved me—she has told me so, and I know, without argument, that she is speaking the truth—yet she found pleasure in the love of another man, and even a certain grim pleasure in his ill-treatment of her. Or should I reverse my order, finding more marvel in her humility under his caresses than under his blows?"

"What am I to believe? that she is cursed with a dual nature, the one coarse and unbridled, the other delicate, conventional, practical, motherly, refined? . . . And is it, can it be, the result of the separate, antagonistic strains in her blood, the southern and the northern legacy? Did she love Westmacott with the one, and me with the other?"[24]

These are surely the questions that V S-W feels have a personal application for her, too.

Heredity and foreign blood were subjects that interested V S-W very much indeed, and these themes occur in several of her books.[25] The reason for her preoccupation with the subject must be that she was acutely aware of her own mixed antecedents. On one side there was the gipsy blood, which, as we shall see,[26] she considered responsible

[21] MS Autobiography, p. 7.
[22] *Heritage*, Collins, London, 1919, pp. 42—3.
[23] *Ibid.*, p. 60.
[24] *Ibid.*, pp. 236—7.
[25] They are: *Heritage*, 1919, *The Dragon in Shallow Waters*, 1921, *Grey Wethers*, 1923, *The Land*, 1926, *The Death of Noble Godavary*, 1932 and *Pepita*, 1937.
[26] Infra, p. 40.

for much of her mother's eccentricity, and of which she was afraid. On the other side there was the Sackville blood, traceable back to the Conquest, the blood that had already produced two poets. She must have felt herself pulled in two directions; wishing to believe in the strength of heredity for the sake of the Sackville blood, and at the same time afraid to do so, because this would have meant that her gipsy blood was equally free to influence her. One moment she rejected the inheritance of her forefathers, the next she was compelled to admit it.

This conflict is clearly illustrated in an unpublished poem which she wrote in February 1928, an extract from which is quoted below. The thoughts contained in the poem were occasioned by her father's death.

> Because I have your eyes
> Does it mean I have your heart?
> No, you are you, I am I,
> Independent and apart.
>
> Violently I refuse
> All seisin with another,
> Be she my kinswoman,
> Be he my own blood-brother.
>
> —Yet stay. Had he that lies
> Dead in the chapel, not
> The same unhappy eyes?
> My father, that me begot?[27]

This concern with her mixed blood and its possible effects on her personality is most noticeable in her early works. 1937 is the last year in which foreign blood appears in her books. With *Pepita,* published the year after Lady Sackville's death, V S-W seems to have become reconciled with her origins, for the subject appears no more.

Duality, the Jekyll and Hyde personality, on the other hand, is frequently present in her works. In only one book, *Devil at Westease,* does this duality actually take the form of one person with two quite different personalities; Professor Warren—kind, gentle and cultivated—and the great, but morally corrupt artist Wyldbore Ryan prove to be one and the same person, although the distance between their two personalities is so great that each speaks and thinks of the other as though he were a separate entity.[28]

V S-W was perfectly aware of the duality of her own nature. In her short autobiography she quotes a comment made by a friend:

"The upper half of your face is so pure and grave,—almost childlike. And the lower half is so domineering, sensual, almost brutal,—it is the most absurd contrast, and extraordinarily symbolical of your Mr. Jekyll and Mr. Hyde personality."[29]

H.N. shows his alarm about the same thing in a letter to V S-W:

What has always worried me is your dual personality. The one tender, wise and with such a sense of responsibility. And the other rather cruel and extravagant. The former has been what I have always clung to as the essential you, but the latter has always alarmed me and I have tried to dismiss it from my mind—or,

[27] The full text of the poem is given on pp. 116—7.
[28] For a more detailed discussion on this book, see infra, pp. 72—3.
[29] MS Autobiography, p. 31.

rather, I have always accepted it as the inevitable counterpart of your remarkable personality.[30]

V S-W must also have been alarmed by the more violent side of her personality. Eighteen months later she wrote what might be regarded as a reply to this letter, although it was actually occasioned by an exhortation from H.N. to give up the attitude that "it is silly to think that anything in life matters much":

> Luckily for you, you have never seen the more tempestuous side of my nature. You have only seen an occasional bubble rising to the surface, which has startled you and made you realise vaguely that I feel passionately, and am vindictive and uncontrollable when my emotions are aroused, but as you do not like that sort of bubble, you have always wisely looked the other way.[31]

The duality of V S-W's nature appears sometimes also to have influenced her in the choice between poetry and prose. Whereas her fiction frequently displays turbulence, strife, and even cruelty and violence, her published poetry and non-fiction is often characterized by what one might call an underlying serenity of spirit, a quality noticeably lacking in the majority of her novels. This is illustrated by the two books that she published in 1921, her second novel, *The Dragon in Shallow Waters*,[32] and her second volume of verse, *Orchard and Vineyard*.[33]

The novel is "a queer tale, ... full of grimness and violence; a tale of two brothers, Gregory and Silas Dene, sinister figures, sprung of a sinister race, whose successive generations seem doomed to bear in some form or other, the marks of physical affliction and mental savagery. Of these brothers, Silas is blind, Gregory deaf and dumb, yet by sheer force of body and character they have established a kind of domination over their fellow villagers".[34] Neither of the brothers is a whole man by himself—each needs the faculties only possessed by his brother in order to become one. They may be taken as representing two sides of a dual personality, an impression strengthened by the fact that they live in the opposite, mirror-image ends of the same double cottage. Gregory is basically a quiet and good man, and is creative—he designs machinery. Silas, on the other hand, is at bottom a violent man and produces nothing, the victim of a "ruthless savagery which always possessed him, without system or goal beyond a need to damage everything that was happy, prosperous, and entire."[35] The conflict which arises because of this duality—Silas envies his brother his creative ability and peace of mind—drives Silas to the murder of his own wife, to inflict senseless suffering on animals, and finally to plan the destruction of Gregory and his wife.

If one turns from this harsh, tortured story, written at about the time when she was going through a personal crisis, to the volume of verse published the same year, one enters a different world. In *Orchard and Vineyard* there is none of the duality which is so obvious in the novel. Strong emotions are not absent,—witness the poems entitled "Dissonance", "Bitterness", and "Insurrection",—but there is a homogeneity about the poems in that they are all spoken by what is recognizably the same voice, albeit in different tones.

One can trace a tendency to keep the two aspects of her personality in two separate compartments; the disharmonic fiction on one side and the more harmonic poetry and non-fiction on the other. It seems unlikely to be a mere coincidence. V S-W's attitude

---

[30] *Diaries and Letters, 1939—45*, p. 157.
[31] *Ibid.*, p. 266.
[32] Collins, London.
[33] John Lane, The Bodley Head, London.
[34] *Times Literary Supplement*, 16 June, 1921, p. 386.
[35] *The Dragon in Shallow Waters*, p. 107.

to what she wrote seems to indicate that she always placed a far higher value on her poetry than on her fiction. When, for example, in 1950, after a long period during which she had felt "really rather depressed by my inability to write the simplest thing",[36] she had again started writing and was at work on a novel, the delight she felt was tempered by a regret that it was prose, not poetry, that had come back to her.

> Darling, I must write you another little note just to say how happy I am writing. It does make the whole difference in life. I just tell you this, because I like sharing things with you. I have been so miserable in the last two or three years not being able to write; really worried I have been, thinking that it was gone from me for ever. I don't mean by this that I think my novel [The Easter Party] will be any good—you know that I am not a good novelist—but at any rate it is exciting just doing it. It keeps me alive, living in an imaginary world which seems more real than the ordinary world. Of course I would rather write poetry. Perhaps that will also return to me one day.[37]

Another indication of the probability that V S-W regarded her poetry as being more important than her other writing is contained in an article written by Jacques Vallette in the *Mercure de France* in 1949. His remarks have the appearance of being based on some personal communication between him and V S-W:

> Elle a écrit en prose des biographies de saintes, l'histoire de sa grand-mère espagnole (*Pepita*), un roman (*The Edwardians*), de longues nouvelles (*All Passion Spent*). Mais elle s'estime surtout poète et veut être jugée sur une collection de vers écrits entre 1913 et la dernière guerre, auxquels s'est ajoutée en 1946 une autre séquence, *The Garden*.[38]

V S-W's attitude to her novels is expressed very clearly in an interview she granted to a representative of the press in October 1930, not long after *The Edwardians* had been published. When asked what she preferred writing, she replied:

> "Poetry every time. I only took to writing prose to fill up the gaps in between poetry writing. I now rather wish I never had! And I wish I could make a bonfire of all my novels . . . I don't like any of my books. Some I dislike more than others, but I can't say I like any of them. I particularly dislike my novels. The only one I can tolerate at all is *Seducers in Ecuador*. I prefer the poetry, books of travel and criticism."[39]

As V S-W clearly valued her poetry higher than her prose, and as she was well aware of the darker side of her nature, it does not seem unreasonable to suppose that she gave freer rein to her conflicting emotions in her fiction in order to be in a calmer frame of mind to write the works to which she attached more importance. Her fiction writing might be described as a sort of catharsis.

In 1920, H.N. left Paris, having completed his work at the Peace Conference. On his return he was appointed to a post at the Foreign Office in London, where he was to remain for the next four and a half years. During this time he and V S-W were living in Pimlico. In the summer, however, V S-W and the children moved down to Long Barn while H.N. continued to stay in London during the week, returning to Long Barn every week-end. One result of this arrangement was the continuation of the correspondence that flowed between them, a custom that had begun with their engagement in 1911 and was to continue until V S-W's death in 1962. Every day that they were

---

[36] *Diaries and Letters, 1945—62*, p. 183.
[37] *Ibid.*, pp. 195—6.
[38] "Victoria Sackville-West", *Mercure de France*, 1—III—1949, pp. 423—4.
[39] *Everyman*, 23 October, 1930, p. 392.

apart each of them wrote to the other, and each kept all the other's letters.[40] Each also kept a diary, but whereas H.N.'s was copious and informative, V S-W's contains little but a list of her engagements and a few quite ordinary comments. She was not the person to communicate her innermost thoughts to an ordinary diary except in rare instances.

In 1922, V S-W published two works. In May, came *The Heir*,[41] containing the long short-story which gives the book its title, and four short-stories entitled: "The Christmas Party", "Patience", "Her Son", and "The Parrot".

"The Heir", with the sub-title "A Love Story", is the first expression of a theme that is to appear in other works by V S-W—the power of a house to affect a person's heart and outlook. The real hero of the story is not Mr Peregrine Chase, the manager of a small insurance office in Wolverhampton, but Blackboys, the beautiful Elizabethan manor which has been left to him by the aunt he never met. He is persuaded to sell the house and estate in order to pay off the mortgages and have a small income left for his own use. Running through the story is a deep feeling of tradition, which the house and its contents symbolize. The influence of this, together with the sheer beauty of the house itself and its setting, work upon Chase until, almost despite himself, he is compelled to attend the auction and, at the eleventh hour, outbid the wealthy Brazilian whose bid would have given Chase financial security, though not Blackboys, for the rest of his life. Blackboys is Knole in a light disguise, and the story is dedicated to B.M., who is Lady Sackville [Bonne Mama].[42]

The last short-story in the volume, "The Parrot", is of considerable interest and has obvious personal applications. The bird in the story is kept in Pimlico, far from its native Uruguay, in a cage from which it is perpetually endeavouring to escape—indeed, it has twice succeeded in doing so. The motives given by the family for not releasing the bird are of the purest; they wish to protect it from cats, dogs, the English climate; but the bird will not understand. The poor little inefficient, downtrodden skivvy whose task it is to look after the parrot has transformed it into a symbol; her fifteen minutes with the bird each day are "the one fabulous excursion of her day; it was a journey to Bagdad, a peep into the caves of Aladdin. 'Casting down their golden crowns upon a glassy sea,' she murmured, in a hotch-potch of religion and romance."[43] Then, one day, "the parrot no longer tore at its bars or screamed, and as for the under-housemaid, she was a transformed creature: punctual, orderly, competent, and unobtrusive. . . . It would have been hypercritical to complain that the girl's quietness was disconcerting."[44] Soon afterwards, having left a note to say that she has gone to wear the golden crown, the girl is found dead on her bed, and the parrot dead in its cage.

The story is dedicated "To H.G.N."—V S-W's husband—and it must have been written some time about the end of 1921, very soon after the crisis in their married life. One can hardly doubt that the parrot represents V S-W herself, as does the skivvy, and that the transmuted symbol of the parrot is a glimpse of the splendour that reveals itself to the vision of a poet. How can H.N. have interpreted this story other than as a warning of what might be the consequences of any interference with her liberty?

The second book that V S-W published in 1922, in the late autumn, was *Knole and the Sackvilles*. This, her first work of non-fiction, was on the whole well received by

[40] *Diaries and Letters, 1930—39*, p. 16.
[41] Heinemann, London, 1922.
[42] See *Diaries and Letters, 1930—39*, p. 35, note 2.
[43] *The Heir*, p. 247.
[44] *Ibid.*, pp. 248—9.

the press. "No one, it is tempting to believe, but a direct descendant of this ancient and distinguished family could have written with so sure and delicate a sympathy the history of its noble house,"[45] said one critic, and praised it for the fact that "to the gift of beautiful English she has joined the quality of imaginative penetration into the past."[46] However, one critic could find fault with it on the grounds that "Miss Sackville-West is a novelist of some distinction and much promise," and that "Miss Sackville-West has left herself entirely out of the book. ... The book is charming, but, charming though it is, we shall be glad to see Miss Sackville-West return to her novel-writing."[47]

It is not strictly true to say that V S-W left herself entirely out of the book—she has in fact included quite a few details of her life as a child—but if a reason is needed why she did not put in more, one need only consider the strength of her feelings for Knole to realise that it might have been too painful for her to do so, as the two stanzas of the unpublished poem given below may show:

Knole, when I went from you, you missed
One of your many children, specially?
God knows I gave you all my love, my agony,
Scarcely a stone of you I had not kissed.

Knole! Knole! I stretch my hands to you in prayer,
You, grey and solid; you, enduring, staid;
You do not know what surges beat against your walls;
Miss me a little, I who am your soul.[48]

One of the important consequences of publishing *Knole and the Sackvilles* was that it led to V S-W making the acquaintance of Virginia Woolf who, after reading the reviews, had written to the author. V S-W had sent her a copy of the book and had promised her a copy of her poems too, whereupon Virginia Woolf wrote:

I should never have dared to dun you if I had known the magnificence of the book. ... There is nothing I enjoy more than family histories, and I am falling upon Knole the first moment I get.

I am shameless enough to hope that the poems won't go to the wrong address.

I was prepared to sniff at Eddie's Georgians,[49] and so I did: but not at yours.

I wonder if you would come and dine with us? Say Monday 8th, 7.45.

We don't dine so much as picnic, as the press has got into the larder and into the dining room, and we never dress.[50]

This was the beginning of a long and intimate friendship between V S-W and Virginia Woolf which lasted until the latter's death in March 1941. It was to prove fruitful to them both.

In 1923 V S-W published three books. They were *The Diary of Lady Anne Clifford*[51] and two novels: *Grey Wethers*[52] and *Challenge*.[53]

The first of these is an edited version of the diary of one of her ancestors. Daughter

[45] *Nation and Athenaeum,* 6 January, 1923, p. 553.
[46] *Ibid.,* p. 554.
[47] *Spectator, Literary Supplement,* 10 February, 1923, p. 218.
[48] The complete poem will be found on pp. 114—5 infra.
[49] *Georgian Poetry,* ed. Edward Marsh, London, 1922.
[50] Unpublished letter dated 3 Jan., 1923, in the possession of Mr Nigel Nicolson.
[51] Heinemann, London.
[52] Heinemann, London.
[53] George Doran, New York.

to the 3rd Earl of Cumberland, Lady Anne married in 1609 Richard, 3rd Earl of Dorset, the grandson of Thomas Sackville. A brief life of Lady Anne is included in *Knole and the Sackvilles,*[54] but as this colourful and strong-willed woman had left a singularly detailed record of her long life, V S-W decided to edit it, publish it separately, and supply it with a long foreword.[55]

Grey Wethers is an exceedingly interesting book to the student of V S-W. It is the story of Clare Warrener, the daughter of a scholarly squire, and her tragic love for Nicolas Lovel, a gipsy. Their tragedy "stands as instance and symbol of a more general theme—the conflict between powers of nature and those of culture and civilization."[56] The setting, which is important to the story, is the heart of the Wiltshire Downs; a little village entirely surrounded by a prehistoric earthwork at the foot of what is, in actual fact, Silbury Hill. In the village stand the sarsen stones, the Grey Wethers.

There is a magical atmosphere about the whole story. The Downs themselves, Starvecrow, the house owned by Calladine, the man Clare eventually marries, the scenes enacted in the snow, are all surrounded by a supernatural aura:

> . . . an enchanted village built round the great monoliths called the Grey Wethers.
> . . . Everyone in King's Avon is under a spell; fantastic figures, unreal as a dream,
> mumble and mutter through the story. The lovers, Clare and Nicholas—he a
> simple village yokel, she a maid of high degree—the most unreal of all, move to-
> gether, are separated, seek each other in the end and are united and mysteriously
> lost to the world that had known them. What became of them the reader is left
> to imagine 'in the manner best suited to his own fancy and requirements'.[57]

The book also owes a debt to *Wuthering Heights,* which has clearly both provided the inspiration and influenced the development of the story.[58] Clare, Lovel and Calladine might well be regarded as V S-W's Catherine, Heathcliff and Edgar Linton, and, as in *Wuthering Heights,* the landscape forms an integral part of the story; the Downs exert an influence on all who live in their shadow. V S-W has, however, adapted the story to suit her own needs. In Lovel and Clare (the name is symbolic: *claire*) she has introduced her own duality. "He was the darkness of the Downs, their threat, their solitude, their intractability; she was their light, their windiness, their sunlit flanks, their springiness of turf. United they formed a whole."[59] This is stressed twice in the book.[60] Symbolic of this duality, too, is Olver's mirror—one of the oldest symbols in the world of magic—in which, he says, each of them can see the image of the other.

In Calladine, V S-W seems, consciously or unconsciously, to have drawn upon and exaggerated all the negative characteristics which might be attributed to H.N.[61] "He was a believer in dilettantism; but in the name of all good taste let it be dilettantism in graceful and becoming subjects."[62] Furthermore, he "appeared satisfied, living with

---

[54] Pp. 60—85.
[55] A description of Lady Anne's life together with extracts from her diary and other writings by her will be found in Phillips, *op. cit.,* I, 276—88. See also the *Complete Peerage,* III (1913), 295—7, and *D.N.B.,* XI (1887), 56—7.
[56] *Spectator,* CXXXI (11 August, 1923), 197.
[57] *Times Literary Supplement,* 23 June, 1923, p. 438.
[58] The only two pictures in V S-W's study were a portrait of Virginia Woolf and a reproduction of Branwell Brontë's painting of his sisters.
[59] *Grey Wethers,* p. 280.
[60] *Ibid.,* p. 81: "In essence, they were equal; different of course, he male, she female, but united they made a whole, each contributing an equal share."
[61] *Grey Wethers* was probably the first novel she wrote after the crisis of 1920. These passages seem to indicate how serious the crisis was, and how long the after-effects lasted. See also V S-W's remarks on her character quoted on p. 35 supra.
[62] *Ibid.,* p. 198.

Clare a captive under his roof."[63] The motif of the bird in the cage, which was so prominent in "The Parrot",[64] is here repeated. Clare's thoughts constantly wander away from Calladine to the freedom of the Downs outside, and Calladine reproaches her:

> Always looking out Clare? what liberty do·you see out there? you think I ought
> to let you go, little caged bird, but you would soon perish,—your pretty little limbs
> wouldn't stand the cold,—better stay happily where you are, believe me,—don't
> fret,—come back to me,—let me whisper how precious you are,—come back to
> our lovely idleness.[65]

In *Grey Wethers* reappears the motif of the northern and the southern blood, first introduced in *Heritage,* this time in two physically separated characters, and again the southern blood is represented as being something to be regarded with suspicion, even shame. Lovel "had before him constantly the sight of his mother and brother to uphold him in the resolution that with the three of them the race must end. Such blood must not be carried on."[66] This motif is also touched upon in *The Land,*[67] here, too, with a feeling of revulsion:

> And then I came to a field where the springing grass
> Was dulled by the hanging cups of fritillaries,
> Sullen and foreign-looking, the snaky flower,
> Scarfed in dull purple, like Egyptian girls
> Camping among the furze, staining the waste
> With foreign colour, sulky-dark and quaint,
> Dangerous too, as a girl might sidle up,
> An Egyptian girl, with an ancient snaring spell,
> Throwing a net, soft round the limbs and heart,
> . . .
> A gipsy Judith, witch of a ragged tent,
> And I shrank from the English field of fritillaries
> Before it should be too late, before I forgot
> The cherry white in the woods, and the curdled clouds,
> And the lapwings crying free above the plough.[68]

The third book V S-W published in 1923, *Challenge,*[69] appeared only in the United States, as there were private reasons why it should not be published in England.[70] The *New York Times* considered the novel "one of the best that V. Sackville-West has written" and described it as:

> A novel of the fine ardor and recklessness of youth and it is placed against a
> pseudo-historical background. The career of Julian Davenant, the young Englishman, affords V. Sackville-West opportunity for the fine mingling of two strains of
> action. First there is that colorful rendering of life on one of the Greek Islands,
> and, secondly, there is the more objective love affair of Julian and Eve, an affair
> that has its tragic implications but which is compact with the passion of youth.
> No possible notice of *Challenge* may be written without emphasis on the fine prose

[63] *Ibid.,* p. 201.
[64] See supra, p. 37.
[65] *Ibid.,* p. 263.
[66] *Ibid.,* p. 100.
[67] William Heinemann, London, 1926.
[68] *The Land,* pp. 49—50.
[69] George H. Doran, New York, 1923.
[70] Letter dated 30/11/70 from Mr Nigel Nicolson to the present author.

employed by the author, for there are times when it moves with an almost lyrical note. The subject matter is assuredly worthy of this method of narrative.[71]

In 1924 appeared the first result of V S-W's growing intimacy with Virginia Woolf. She had agreed that the Hogarth Press should publish her next book, and on 7th June Virginia Woolf, who was anxious to know when it would be ready, wrote to say that "it is very good news that your story may be ready by July, or is it a poem?" By the 15th September the manuscript was in Virginia Woolf's hands, and she had read it, for she wrote on that day to V S-W to let her have her reactions:

> It is not, of course, altogether thrust through; I think it could be tightened up, and aimed straighter, but there is nothing to spoil it in this. I like its texture—the sense of all the fine things you have dropped into it, so that it is full of beauty in itself when nothing is happening. Nevertheless such interesting things do happen, so suddenly—barely too. And I like its objectivity so that one can play about with it—interpret it different ways. ... I am very glad we are going to publish it, and extremely proud and indeed touched, with my childlike dazzled affection for you, that you should dedicate it to me.[72]

The book was *Seducers in Ecuador*,[73] a short work of only seventy-four pages in a style that is reminiscent of that in the short-stories of Henry James.[74] In the opinion of one critic:

> What the tale fixes on as really devastating is the unlicensed spirit of imagination, which is never more hazardous than when it is conjured up by ordinary people.[75]

The story is treated in a surrealistic manner throughout, the tone being set by Lomax's tinted spectacles, for "with a rapidity that he was never well able to understand, he found himself in such a position that he no longer dared to remove his spectacles at all; he could not face a return to the daylight mood; realism was no longer for him."[76]

The first part of the story, from Lomax's marriage to Miss Whitaker up to his promise to Bellamy (note the names), takes place on the latter's yacht, aboard which there is an atmosphere which might be interpreted as slightly homosexual. Much of the action takes place at sea, dissociated from place and, to some extent, from time, which imparts to the story a sense of universality. The last part, on the other hand, is enacted in the court-room and in prison; a concrete reality which Lomax has to go through denuded of his tinted spectacles.

The story might well be described as an illustration of the inevitability with which Fate overtakes her victim, who, in this case, willingly submits to her decree. Miss Whitaker plays the part of the totally insignificant agent who is instrumental in bringing about disaster, in this case through her brother Robert, a shadowy, sinister Nemesis in whose existence Lomax does not believe, for "since Robert existed, what need had she to mention him?"[77] His escape from this Nemesis is rendered impossible by his marriage to Miss Whitaker.

Added point is given to the whole by irony: the woman for whom Lomax has been waiting so long becomes free to marry him on the very day he weds Miss Whitaker; a post-mortem shows that Bellamy has never suffered from any fatal disease; Miss

[71] *New York Times*, Book Review, 18 February, 1923, p. 11.
[72] Pippett, *The Moth and the Star*, Boston, 1955, p. 173.
[73] Hogarth Press, London, 1924.
[74] As regards the influence of other writers on V S-W's style, see infra, pp. 88—9, 100—1.
[75] *Times Literary Supplement*, 27 November, 1924, p. 794.
[76] *Seducers in Ecuador*, p. 10.
[77] *Ibid.*, p. 51.

Whitaker is proved to be a virgin, and Lomax's motives are derided in court; the money Bellamy leaves Lomax, which is instrumental in directing suspicion to him in the first place, is never used for the humanitarian purposes for which Lomax has decreed that it shall be used. But "Lomax at night in his cell was almost happy: he was glad to endure this for Bellamy's sake. He had loved Bellamy."[78] Lomax never resists his fate, is never surprised by the turn events take, and his execution is a sort of sacrificial death to which he willingly submits.

The book is unlike any other V S-W wrote, both in style and in tone. It is the only one of her books that a reader immediately recognizes as presenting difficulties in interpretation. The fact that, up to 1930 at any rate, V S-W herself liked it better than any of her other novels[79] may be due to its very obscurity; she was, as she has stressed, a very secretive person.[80]

In 1925, H.N. was posted to Teheran as Counsellor at the British Embassy. He obviously realized that after having had such a long spell in England at the Foreign Office he would have to spend several years abroad, for he sold the house in Pimlico and V S-W moved permanently down to Long Barn. Although separation was painful to them both, V S-W never considered accompanying H.N. on his tours abroad. To do so would have meant acting as hostess and becoming involved in the social life that she disliked so much.[81] She did, however, pay two short visits to her husband in Teheran; in the spring of 1926 and again a year later. She has described her experiences in two books: *Passenger to Teheran*,[82] and *Twelve Days*.[83]

On her first visit, she travelled to Persia via Egypt and Basrah, whence she proceeded by rail to Bagdad and completed the journey in a car of the Trans-Desert Mail from the frontier of Irak over the mountains to Kermanshah, Kazvin and Teheran. During her nearly two-month-long stay in the country she not only spent a considerable amount of time exploring the capital and its environs, but also made a journey to Isfahan by car.[84]

In Persia she met a way of life that had remained unchanged for centuries, a society on which modern civilization had as yet made almost no impression and in which the craftsman still worked according to his ancient traditions. "But in the meantime the Europeans go on with their tea-parties, and their leaving of cards, and their speculations as to why some one was not to be seen, yesterday, at some one else's house."[85] Her early life and the remembrance of the parties given by her mother at Knole had already left her with a distaste for what she considered the meaningless life of Society and, by contrast, an appreciation of the traditional and significant values which the craftsman and the labourer on the soil stood for. Her experiences in Persia undoubtedly gave renewed force to these prejudices and exerted an influence on *The Land,* which she was then writing,[86] and on *The Edwardians,* published four years later.

Another effect of her stay in Persia was that it brought home to her once again the realisation that places meant so much more to her than people. It caused her some concern, for she thought that:

[78] *Ibid.,* p. 68.
[79] See supra, p. 36.
[80] See supra, p. 20.
[81] *Diaries and Letters, 1930—39,* p. 29.
[82] Hogarth Press, London, 1926.
[83] Hogarth Press, London, 1928.
[84] *Passenger to Teheran,* pp. 107—37.
[85] *Ibid.,* p. 100.
[86] See infra, p. 43.

There must . . . be something a little wrong with some one who attached, instinctively, so much importance to place; . . . These brief but frequent fallings-in-love gave me cause for serious anxiety; such vibrations of response ought, I felt, to be reserved for one's contact with human beings, nor should nature have a greater power than human nature to excite and to stir the soul.[87]

Her second visit to Persia, in 1927, strengthened her prejudices even more. On this occasion V S-W, H.N. and three other Europeans made a journey from Isfahan through the heart of the Bakhtiari Mountains to the Persian oilfields. Apart from the first and the last day's journey, the entire trip was made on foot and by mule. The story is recorded in *Twelve Days*.

Their arrival at the Anglo-Iranian Oil Company's sites produced a feeling of revulsion in V S-W:

The contrast was so great as to produce an almost physical shock. . . . From constant contact with life reduced to its simplest elements, we walked straight into a hell of civilisation. . . . There were grocers' shops with the familiar tins and bottles on the counters; there were schools, and cool, organised hospitals; there were tennis-courts occupied by young women in summer dresses and young men in white flannels. There was, no doubt, society, intrigues, and gossip. One shuddered at the thought of it.[88]

Another discovery she made on this journey, or perhaps first publicly revealed in the account of it, was that she was by nature one of those persons for whom solitude holds no terrors. On the contrary:

I write as one with a strong head for large draughts of solitude. . . . To live encamped even within sight of the Bakhtiari Road, that rude, violent, and occasional highway, would more than satisfy the misanthropy of most people. It would not satisfy mine.[89]

V S-W probably started to write *The Land* about the middle of 1923. She had the admirable habit, when writing long poems, of dating each day's work, and the earliest passage of *The Land,* written down in a one-hundred-page folio notebook obviously bought for the purpose, is dated 5th June, 1923.[90] The first draft of *The Land* shows that, after this date, she added nothing more to the poem until 3rd May, 1924, almost a year later. Even then, however, the poem progressed slowly; a little more was added in June and in November 1924, but then it was laid aside again until the following July. From that time on, the poem progressed more rapidly, and each month saw sections added to it until, on 8th December, 1925, the original version of the poem was complete and was sent to the printers. The proofs are dated 15th January, 1926.[91] When V S-W left for Persia shortly afterwards she must have taken both her notebook and the proofs with her; under the influence of what she experienced in Persia she made quite a few alterations and a number of additions, some of them lengthy, as the notebook and the proofs show. The last date in the notebook is 20th February, and the completed poem is dated Teheran, April 1926.

There are two principal motifs in *The Land*. The first is a detailed and loving record of the age-old ways of English agricultural life made at a time when the old customs

[87] *Ibid.,* p. 123.
[88] *Twelve Days,* p. 121—2.
[89] *Ibid.,* pp. 80—1.
[90] A microfilm of the entire first draft of *The Land* is to be found in the Manuscript Department of the Kungl. Bibliotek in Stockholm, reference No. MfH 349.
[91] In the possession of Mr Nigel Nicolson, Sissinghurst Castle.

were rapidly dying out. As much of what she recorded is in the oral tradition,[92] it is clear that if she had waited another twenty-five years or so before writing the poem, it would hardly have been possible for her to write it in its existing form.

This had become apparent even by 1933, only seven years later, for, in a review of V S-W's *Collected Poems,*[93] which included *The Land,* a critic said that "the truth it tells has become more urgently necessary; the world to which it invites our affections and fancies, being more blatantly threatened, is already more precious."[94]

Richard Church, in an article written on V S-W a few years later, also stresses the great historic importance of the poem:

> *The Land* is a picture of certain aspects of an England which is vanishing; ...
> Our social historians ... have shown us the seamy side of that bucolic scene; the gross brutality, injustice, covert slavery, squalor and filth. But in the bringing of those things to light, our historians have tended to neglect the positive qualities of a countryside held together by the pattern of the Feudal System and the rule-of-thumb Guilds. They have dismissed as superstition much of the lore of the peasant, and have failed to explain the secrets of his craft, secrets that were learned from no Trade Union handbook. They have neglected his personal delight and the simplicity of his relationship with the earth he tilled, the birds and animals he both loved and preyed on, the flowers he sometimes trod underfoot and sometimes set in the window of his mind, the God he worshipped in his village churches and objurgated in his week-day superstitions. It was left for the poets to record those things, and Miss Sackville-West has played a noble part in this preservation of something which is precious, and which is vanishing.[95]

The second characteristic of the poem is V S-W's regard for tradition and the craftsman. Part of this feeling comes from her appreciation of the craftsman as a creative artist, for:

> All craftsmen share a knowledge. They have held
> Reality down fluttering to a bench;
> Cut wood to their own purposes; compelled
> The growth of pattern with the patient shuttle;
> Drained acres to a trench.
> Control is theirs. They have ignored the subtle
> Release of spirit from the jail of shape.
> They have been concerned with prison, not escape;
> Pinioned the fact, and let the rest go free,
> And out of need made inadvertent art.[96]

Part of the feeling came from the pride she felt in her Sackville ancestry; the pride that was so necessary to her to counterbalance the presence of the gipsy blood she was so conscious of. Tradition was particularly important to this side of V S-W.

It was the reverse side of this intense feeling for tradition that made V S-W the unashamed conservative in outlook that she was,—the conservative who could write:

---

[92] Although V S-W experienced difficulty in establishing contact with people (see supra, p. 25), this did not apply to her relationship with servants, etc., as her article entitled "The Edwardians below stairs", *Vogue,* 25 November, 1931, pp. 55—7, shows. She would have had no difficulty in discussing agriculture with farmers.

[93] Hogarth Press, London, 1933.

[94] *Times Literary Supplement,* 30 November, 1933, p. 852.

[95] "V. Sackville-West: A Poet in a Tradition", the *Fortnightly Review* CXLVIII (1940), 603.

[96] *The Land,* p. 81.

My Manifesto: I hate democracy. I hate *la populace.* I wish education had never been introduced. I don't like tyranny, but I like an intelligent oligarchy. I wish *la populace* had never been encouraged to emerge from its rightful place. I should like to see them as well fed and well housed as T.T. cows, but no more articulate than that.[97]

Although one of the reasons why she wrote *The Land* was the realization of the increasing threat of progress to traditional rural life, the poem contains only indirect references to her dislike of modern methods and bustle, such as when she refers to the thatcher, one of the most highly skilled of craftsmen, as:

Brother to all the slow fastidious folk
Whose care is matched by their disdain of time[98]

or exhorts the harvester to:

Be prouder than the punctual rigid clerk,
And stickle not to labour after dark,
For you take nature's orders, he the clock's.[99]

Direct criticism of modern life is not to be found until after her second trip to Persia when, after having lived a primitive life for a fortnight in the Bakhtiari Mountains, she experienced her return to civilization as a terrible shock. In *The Edwardians,* published in 1930, occurs the scene when Sebastian, the young heir to Chevron, finds the head carpenter with his eyes swimming in tears, and is told:

"It's my boy, your Grace—Frank, my eldest. Your Grace knows that I was to have taken him into the shops this year. Well, he won't come. He wants to go— I hardly know how to tell your Grace. He wants to go into the motor trade instead. Says it's the coming thing. Now your Grace knows . . . that my father and his father before him were in the shops, and I looked to my boy to take my place after I was gone. Same as your Grace's son, if I may make the comparison. I never thought to see a son of mine leave Chevron so long as he was fit to stay there. And Frank *is* fit—a neater-handed boy I seldom saw. That's what draws him to engines. Now what is engines, I ask your Grace? What's screwing up a nut beside handling a nice piece of wood? Such nice pieces of wood as I have lying out in the timber-yard, too; will be as ripe as a violin in forty years or so. Just right for Frank to handle by the time he's sixty. . . . I picked the oak for the grain myself" . . . "Frank," I said, "when you're sixty and need a nice piece of wood, you'll find it here, and don't you forget your father put it there for you." And now he wants to go into the motor trade . . . But it seems to me that everything is breaking up, now that my eldest wants to leave the shops and go into the motor trade."[100]

After her return from the second trip to Persia, V S-W wrote a short biographical work: *Aphra Behn: The Incomparable Astrea.*[101] It is not altogether a successful venture, for some of the argument is contradictory and the conclusions are weak. It is interesting, however, for two reasons. Firstly, it is her first essay in this genre, apart from the long foreword she wrote to *The Diary of Lady Anne Clifford,* and secondly, it gives an insight into another of V S-W's own characteristics: her outlook on the rights of women.

V S-W's status as a biographer and the tradition in which she worked are discussed

[97] *Diaries and Letters, 1939—45,* p. 433.
[98] *The Land,* p. 80.
[99] *Ibid.,* p. 72.
[100] *The Edwardians,* pp. 40—1.
[101] Gerald Howe, London, 1927.

in chapter VIII of this dissertation. Let us here consider the probable reason why she chose Aphra Behn as the subject of her first biography. It seems that her choice was governed not so much by the fact that she was in possession of new information, although she had discovered three articles that she considered threw new light on Aphra Behn's early life;[102] nor can it have been because she thought Aphra Behn a great, or even underestimated, writer, for she avows frankly "that Mrs Behn, given her natural talent, prodigally wasted her opportunities".[103] But "the fact that she wrote is more important than the quality of what she wrote. The importance of Aphra Behn is that she was the first woman in England to earn her living by her pen."[104]

Though certainly not a feminist in the accepted sense of the word, V S-W had strong feelings about a woman's right to an independent existence. Dr Bernbaum had made allegations about Aphra Behn which, if true, would have deprived her of a good deal of her glory,[105] and V S-W seems to have been stung by these into defending her.

As far as V S-W herself was concerned, this feeling about a woman's rights took the form of a violent dislike of anything that tended to rob her of her personal identity. For example, she was always very annoyed if she were ever referred to as an authoress or a poetess. H.N. records:

> In the evening we listen to a broadcast by Vita on the Home Service. She is furious because they introduce her as "V. Sackville-West, the well-known authoress". She had managed to persuade them not to call her "Lady Nicolson" or "Miss Sackville-West" or "Miss Victoria Sackville-West", but had omitted to warn them not to put "author" in the feminine.[106]

Above all, however, it was the fact that as a married woman she was officially known by her husband's name that infuriated her. When she had to fill in a passport application form in the name of Mrs Harold Nicolson:

> This, as always, has flung me into a rage. You know I love you more than anybody has ever loved anybody else, but I really do resent being treated as if I were your dog. The whole thing is an insult to human dignity, and ought to be revised. One is allowed no separate existence at all, but merely as a dependent upon whomever one marries. Why not get me a collar with your name and address engraved upon it?[107]

The reason why she felt so strongly about her name is undoubtedly largely connected with her feelings for Knole and her ancestry, as the following extract from an unpublished poem will show:

> I will hold to my own, old name,
> Walled within walls of Knole;
> I will not sink my pride, my soul,
> In another's pride and fame.[108]

Another illustration of the importance to her of her name is the following extract from H.N.'s diary about an appeal she made for the National Trust:

> I go . . . to the recording room . . . just in time to hear Vita announced as Miss

---

[102] H.D. Benjamin, "Een Koninklijke slaav in Suriname", *De West-Indische Gids,* Amsterdam, October 1919; "Nog eens: Aphra Behn", *Ibid.,* February 1921; "Is Aphra Behn in Suriname geweest?", *Ibid.,* February 1927.
[103] *Aphra Behn,* p. 72.
[104] *Ibid.,* p. 12.
[105] Ernest Bernbaum, "Mrs Behn's Biography a Fiction", *Kittredge Anniversary Papers,* 1913.
[106] *Diaries and Letters, 1945—62,* pp. 385—6.
[107] *Ibid.,* p. 71.
[108] MS in the possession of Mr Nigel Nicolson. For the full text of the poem see pp. 115—6 infra.

Victoria S-W. I expect a row, but she does her piece with swan-like calm. Only at the end, when she has to give her name and address, does she fling into the initial "V" all the loathing which she has of her full name, or of my name, or of any name except V. S-W.[109]

Her extension of this dislike to include being referred to as an authoress or poetess is merely the logical consequence of this.

In 1928 Virginia Woolf published *Orlando*. She had begun to think of writing some book on an entirely new pattern as early as June 1925,[110] perhaps as a result of Lytton Strachey's suggestion that she should try "something wilder and more fantastic [than *Mrs Dalloway*], a framework that admits of anything, like *Tristram Shandy*",[111] but had done little more than think about it until October 1927. By 22nd October that year, however, she was able to note in her diary: "I am writing *Orlando* half in a mock style very clear and plain, so that people will understand every word. But the balance between truth and fantasy must be careful. It is based on Vita, Violet Trefusis, Lord Lascelles, Knole, etc."[112]

When published, the book had the sub-title "A Biography", but it is so only in the sense that it endeavours to catch the essence of the people it is about, and it does not concern itself to any great extent with biographical detail. Orlando's life is narrated from the reign of Queen Eliabeth, when he was a young nobleman, up to the present day. About the end of the seventeenth century, however, Orlando suddenly finds that he has become a woman, which he remains in form until the end of the book. In the things that happen to Orlando, and the feelings that he/she experiences, the initiated reader will recognize all the significant events of V S-W's life, including her marriage to H.N.,—Marmaduke Bonthrop Shelmerdine Esq—observed and interpreted through the eyes of Virginia Woolf.

The following passage occurs in Herbert Marder's book on Virginia Woolf:

> Orlando and her husband Shelmardine [sic], on the other hand, are truly androgynous, the two sexes within them almost evenly balanced. It is because of the fineness of the balance that Orlando must constantly be shifting back and forth, that is, conforming her outer sex to changes in the inner weather. For the dramatic change of sex is only the first of many changes that follow without fanfare. The state of things becomes apparent shortly after Orlando's transformation into a woman.[113]

Marder then goes on to quote the words of the narrator of the story, who finds that "she [Orlando] was censuring both sexes equally, as if she belonged to neither; and indeed, for the time being, she seemed to vacillate; she was man; she was woman; she knew the secrets, shared the weaknesses of each. It was a most bewildering and whirligig state of mind to be in".[114]

There is in James Hafley's interpretation of Virginia Woolf as a novelist an interesting comment on the fact that Orlando and Shelmerdine are from the first moment in such perfect communion with each other:

> The mentally androgynous man and woman can understand each other with a perfection impossible to those barred behind the limitations of their sex. When

[109] *Diaries and Letters, 1945—62,* p. 72.
[110] Virginia Woolf, *A Writer's Diary,* London, 1954, p. 80.
[111] *Ibid.,* p. 79.
[112] *Ibid.,* p. 117.
[113] *Feminism and Art,* Chicago, 1968, pp. 115—6.
[114] *Orlando,* p. 145.

Orlando and Marmaduke meet, they understand each other immediately: "An awful suspicion rushed into both their minds simultaneously:

  'You're a woman, Shel!' she cried.

  'You're a man, Orlando!' he cried."

The truth is that both are androgynous.[115]

If Hafley is correct, Virginia Woolf's view would account for much that would otherwise be difficult to explain in the life of V S-W and H.N.

Andrew Marvell was a poet who interested V S-W, partly because he "was open to *direct* inspiration. . . . The source of his direct inspiration was nature; orderly, detailed nature; nature as he saw it in England." This interest was heightened because, although he lived in an age in which "flashes of personal intimacy and the desire for identification with nature were common to English poets in Marvell's age, as in nearly every other,"[116] there was nevertheless a difference between him and his contemporaries:

  To Marvell, in the brief years of his poetic creation, the mood was constant. . . .
  Conceits, when they occurred, were an ornament—or shall I say a disfigurement?
  —rather than an integral part; his real mood, in these nature poems, was the mood
  of seeing, and feeling; the mysticism which arose as their accompaniment was no
  conceit, but an inevitable consequence, familiar to everyone who has ever entered
  into a moment of communion with nature; and, as such, expressed by him in a
  manner readily distinguishable from the cerebral exertions of his colleagues.[117]

Here V S-W stresses the significance of the spirit of an age. After saying that "it was not to be expected that Marvell should go free of conceits and 'wit', or that he should resist the temptations of screwing his mind round into the prevailing contortions in the pursuit of some over-complicated and over-subtle conception of the universe or of his own consciousness," she explains her meaning by adding: "So strong, so instinctive, is the habit of mind of one's own age, that the conceits of the metaphysical poets—to us frequently so tortured and so extravagant—to them formed an intrinsic part of the process of poetic expression."[118]

It is now possible to see more fully why Marvell should have such a strong attraction for V S-W. She, too, was open to direct inspiration from nature as she saw it in England, as she considered Marvell had been, and, like him, she was a poet not altogether in harmony with the habit of mind of her own age:

  What worries me a bit is being so out of touch with poetry as it is being written
  today. I see that the influence of Tom Eliot and the Spender-Auden school is
  paramount, yet I cannot get into gear with it at all. It is just something left out
  of my make-up.[119]

In 1927, H.N. was transferred from Teheran to Berlin. Once again V S-W refused to accompany him; she remained at Long Barn, writing. H.N. was making a success of his career as a diplomatist. At Berlin he was the second-ranking official at an important Embassy where, for a time, he acted as Chargé d'Affaires.[120] If he continued in the Service he could be sure of getting an Embassy sooner or later. On the other hand,

[115] *The Glass Roof: Virginia Woolf as Novelist,* Berkeley, 1954, p. 104.
[116] *Andrew Marvell,* Faber & Faber, London, 1929, pp. 32—3.
[117] *Ibid.,* pp. 33—4.
[118] *Ibid.,* p. 27.
[119] *Diaries and Letters, 1945—62,* p. 38.
[120] *Diaries and Letters, 1930—39,* p. 29.

much as he loved his work, he realised that it would inevitably entail a future with many years of enforced separation from V S-W.

In 1921 H.N. had started to write books. By 1927 he had published one novel,[121] four works of literary biography, one of general biography and one on the development of English biography.[122] Moreover, friends in England, notably Leonard and Virginia Woolf, had told him that he was wasting his talents in diplomacy; he should be a writer or enter politics.[123] There were, however, certain impediments against taking either of these courses. One of them was that Lady Sackville had been paying V S-W the sum of £1,600 a year under a trust settlement made when they were married. With increasing age, however, Lady Sackville was becoming more and more eccentric[124] at times being quite capable of accusing the Nicolsons of stealing her furniture, her jewels or her money, or of refusing to allow her to place a wreath on Lord Sackville's grave.[125] H.N. and V S-W therefore wished to renounce this settlement, but as a civil servant, his salary would not have been large enough for them to do so; nor could authorship alone guarantee him an income large enough to make them independent of Lady Sackville were he to leave the diplomatic service. For the time being the only possible course was to continue as they were.

From time to time H.N. came home on leave, but at the end of each period came the anguish of parting. This anguish was greatest for V S-W. It is probably true of her to say that she could give H.N. only one side of her love, but for her that was the vitally important one—the light side of her nature—and she gave it to him completely and without stint. With the passing of the years her love for him grew stronger, and each parting more painful. On 25th June, 1929 she was moved to write in a long letter after coming home from seeing him off at the station:

What is so torturing when I leave you at these London stations and drive off, is the knowledge that you are *still there*—that, for half an hour or three-quarters of an hour, I could still return and find you . . .

I came straight home, feeling horribly desolate and sad, driving down that familiar and dreary road. I remembered Rasht and our parting there; our parting at Victoria when you left for Persia; till our life seemed made up of partings, and I wondered how long it would continue . . .

Then I came home, and it was no consolation at all. You see, when I am unhappy for other reasons, the cottage is a real solace to me; but when it is on account of *you* that I am unhappy (because you have gone away), it is an additional pang—it is the same place, but a sort of mockery and emptiness hangs about it—I almost wish that just *once* you could lose me and then come straight back to the cottage and find it still full of me but empty of me, then you would know what I go through after you have gone away . . .

You are dearer to me than anybody ever has been or ever could be. If you died suddenly, I should kill myself as soon as I had made provision for the boys. I really mean this. I could not live if I lost you. I do not think one could conceive of a love more exclusive, more tender, or more pure than I have for you. I think it is immortal, a thing which happens seldom.

[121] *Sweet Waters*, Constable, London, 1921.
[122] *Paul Verlaine*, Constable, London, 1921; *Tennyson*, Constable, 1923; *Byron: The Last Journey*, Constable, 1924; *Swinburne*, Macmillan, London, 1927; *Some People*, Constable, 1927; *The Development of English Biography*, Hogarth Press, London, 1927.
[123] *Diaries and Letters, 1930—39*, p. 32.
[124] *Ibid.*, p. 34.
[125] *Ibid.*, p. 34.

Darling, there are not many people who would write such a letter after sixteen years of marriage, yet who would be saying therein only one-fiftieth of what they were feeling as they wrote it. I sometimes try to tell you the truth, and then I find that I have no words at my command which could possibly convey it to you.[126]

When, a month later, H.N. was told that Lord Beaverbrook, who was looking for a suitable man to edit a page like the Londoner's Diary in the *Evening Standard*, had said that he would be interested in retaining him at a salary of £3,000 a year which could be supplemented by outside literary work,[127] H.N. felt that the matter should be given serious consideration.

It was a difficult decision to make. Against the certainty of success in the Diplomatic Corps, which he loved, he had to place the uncertainty of the newspaper world and his doubts as to whether he would feel at home with the sort of writing he would be expected to do there, but also the chance of being able to live in England and free himself from the necessity of accepting Lady Sackville's endowment. In September he decided to accept Beaverbrook's offer and handed in his resignation to the Foreign Office. On 20th December, 1929, he left Berlin and on 1st January the following year he began work at the *Evening Standard*.[128]

The years 1913 to 1929 were the years in which V S-W learnt to know herself. They show her consciousness of the duality within her, and how this duality is reflected in her works. They show the development of her complex relationship with H.N., passing through a crisis in 1920 to her realisation of the nature and the depth of the love she bore him. They show her concern with her heredity and how it affected her writing. They are the years in which she developed from an immature, complex-ridden girl to a mature woman with a strong and distinctive character.

[126] *Ibid.*, pp. 33—4.
[127] *Ibid.*, p. 34.
[128] *Ibid.*, p. 36.

The Years 1930 to 1946

When H.N. joined the staff of the *Evening Standard* on 1st January, 1930, a great change took place in the Nicolsons' lives. In the first place, in order to be near his office, H.N. took chambers in London in February; No 4, King's Bench Walk, in the Inner Temple. There he and V S-W lived during the week for the next few months, returning to Long Barn at the week-ends. This they were able to do as both their sons were at boarding school by this time; Benedict, aged 15, was at Eton, and Nigel, aged 12, at Summer Fields, Oxford.[1]

In the middle of March that year a disturbing rumour reached them that the property next to Long Barn was to be sold to a large poultry firm. Faced with this threat to their neighbouring fields, the Nicolsons first tried to buy the land themselves, but as the price was high, they decided to look around the Weald of Kent and Sussex for another house where they could live unmolested. On 4th April "Vita telephones to say she has seen the ideal house—a place in Kent near Cranbrook, a sixteenth-century castle"[2] and the following day the whole family went to have a look at it. When they re-visited the castle the following day they decided to consider buying it.

Sissinghurst Castle had once been a great Tudor mansion, the home of Sir John Baker in the reign of Henry VIII. It was his daughter, Cecily, who had married Thomas Sackville in 1554. The castle had deteriorated since the middle of the 18th century, when Horace Walpole had described it as "a house in ruins and a park in ten times greater ruins"[3]. Four years after his visit, it was leased to the Government as a prison for French sailors captured in the Seven Years War. Sissinghurst had never recovered from that experience; a large part of it had been pulled down about 1800, and for nearly sixty years after that, the remaining buildings had been used as the parish workhouse. Since 1845 it had been a romantic, if neglected, adjunct to a farm. Some of the surviving buildings had been used as stables and outhouses, others as dwellings for farm labourers. When H.N. and V S-W looked at it, there was not a single room that they could immediately occupy and the garden was a vast rubbish heap.[4]

It was a depressing sight, and a great deal of imagination must have been needed to see what could be made of it. H.N.'s mother, Lady Carnock, was very much against the idea when she saw it a few days later, which caused H.N. and V S-W to hesitate for some time before deciding to buy it. But on 24th April H.N. wrote V S-W a letter which finally settled the matter in their minds.

[1] *Diaries and Letters, 1930—39*, p. 39—40.
[2] *Ibid.*, p. 44.
[3] *Ibid.*, pp. 43, 425.
[4] *Ibid.*, p. 43.

My view is:

(a) That it is most unwise of us to get Sissinghurst. It costs us £12,000 to buy and will cost another good £15,000 to put it in order. This will mean nearly £30,000 before we have done with it. For £30,000 we could buy a beautiful place replete with park, garage, h. and c., central heating, historical associations, and two lodges r. and l.

(b) That it is most wise of us to buy Sissinghurst. Through its veins pulses the blood of the Sackville dynasty. True it is that it comes through the female line— but then we are both feminist and, after all, Knole came in the same way. It is, for you, an ancestral mansion: that makes up for the company's water and h. and c.

(c) It is in Kent. It is in a part of Kent we like. It is self-contained. I could make a lake. The boys could ride.

(d) We like it.[5]

A fortnight later, on 7th May, they bought it.

Of the two, it was certainly V S-W who was the driving force behind making the decision to buy the castle. She had wanted Sissinghurst from the first moment she saw it, partly, no doubt, because she saw what could be done with it, ruin though it was, but the main reason was almost certainly another. Two years before this, she had finally lost any hope she may have had of keeping Knole. Her father had died in February 1928, and her uncle, Charles Sackville-West, had succeeded to both Knole and the title. She must have felt that is was no longer 'her home and did not, in fact, visit Knole again until 1961, shortly before her death.[6] H.N. pinpointed the real reason for her eagerness to buy Sissinghurst when he wrote "Through its veins pulses the blood of the Sackville dynasty. . . . It is, for you, an ancestral mansion."[7]

Having bought Sissinghurst, H.N. and V S-W threw themselves with great energy into the task of putting the grounds and the buildings to rights. There was an immense amount to be done just to make the existing buildings habitable, for they were all in a state of considerable dilapidation; it was not until October 1930 that they were able to sleep there. But H.N. and V S-W also planned to transform the grounds into something that was to become one of the show gardens of England. A start on this project was made early in 1931,[8] but it was not until the end of 1937 that the bulk of the work was finished.[9]

After the rootless years which followed her marriage to H.N. and the subsequent departure from Knole, years during which she had not been living at any place to which she could feel that she had any permanent attachment, the purchase of Sissinghurst must have been very important to V S-W. It was not only that the castle gave her a link with the past, a sort of replacement for Knole; the work of creating a garden gave her a purpose in life, apart from her writing, which could keep her fully occupied at a time of life which might otherwise have proved difficult for her. Leonard Woolf has summed up well how much the garden at Sissinghurst meant to V S-W:

As the thousands of people who every year visit Sissinghurst know, she restored a good deal of the castle and created a garden of very great beauty.

In the creation of Sissinghurst and its garden she was, I think, one of the happiest people I have ever known, for she loved them and they gave her complete

[5] *Ibid.*, pp. 47—8.
[6] *Diaries and Letters, 1945—62*, p. 391.
[7] *Diaries and Letters, 1930—39*, p. 47.
[8] *Ibid.*, p. 68, 78.
[9] *Ibid.*, p. 425.

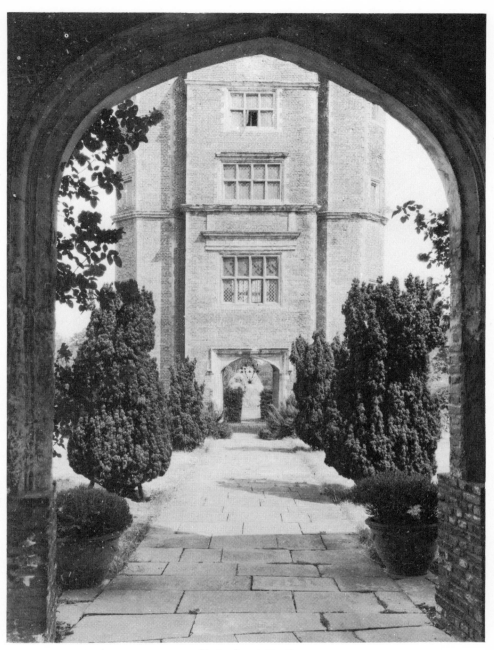

Sissinghurst Castle

satisfaction in the long years between middle age and death in which for so many people when they look out of the windows there is only darkness and desire fails.[10]

V S-W described her own feelings in the short poem *Sissinghurst,*[11] written in 1930. She is "a tired swimmer in the waves of time"[12] and has found:

> . . . the castle and the rose.
> Buried in time and sleep,
> So drowsy, overgrown,
> That here the moss is green upon the stone,
> And lichen stains the keep.

She was able to identify herself with the castle in a way that she had never been able to do with other places at which she had lived since her marriage because of its connection with the Sackvilles, "by birthright, far from present fashion".

In these surroundings she could escape from the modern world and "sink down through centuries to another clime", to a sanctuary which seemed:

> . . . an image, water-drowned,
> Where stirs no wind and penetrates no sound,
> Illusive, fragile to a touch, remote,
> Foundered within the well of years as deep
> As in the waters of a stagnant moat.
> . . .
> As no disturber of the mirrored trance
> I move, and to the world above the waters
>   Wave my incognisance.

In the security given her by the castle, and surrounded by the age-old methods of agriculture which meant so much to her, she feels capable of recovering from the loss of Knole and creating something anew:

> Beauty, and use, and beauty once again
> Link up my scattered heart, and shape a scheme
> Commensurate with a frustrated dream.

Although V S-W never recovered completely from the loss of Knole, she developed an almost equally strong and very possessive love of Sissinghurst. In 1958, for instance, she cut H.N. out of the running of the castle, which was to be entirely hers,[13] and her reactions when she heard that Nigel Nicolson had discussed the possibility of one day handing Sissinghurst over to the National Trust were almost hysterical:

> H. said that Nigel had sounded him on whether I would ever consider giving Sissinghurst to the National Trust. I said, Never, never, never! *Au grand jamais, jamais.* Never, never, never! Not that hard little metal plate at my door! Nigel can do what he likes when I am dead, but so long as I live, no National Trust or any other foreign body shall have my darling. No, no. Over my corpse or my ashes, not otherwise. No, no. I felt myself flush with rage. It is bad enough to have lost my

---

[10] *Downhill All The Way*, Hogarth Press, London, p. 113.
[11] Hogarth Press, London, 1931. Reprinted in *Collected Poems*, pp. 111—4.
[12] This and the following quotations are all from the first 64 lines of *Sissinghurst.*
[13] *Diaries and Letters, 1945—62*, p. 352. Also a letter dated 1/1/71 from Mr Nigel Nicolson to the present author.

Knole, but they shan't take Sissinghurst from me. That at least is my own. *Il y a des choses qu'on peut pas supporter*. They shan't; they shan't; I won't. They can't make me. I *won't*. They can't make me. I never would.[14]

In spite of the fact that the restoration of the castle and the creation of a great garden occupied a considerable amount of her time, she does not appear to have devoted less time to her writing than she did before, for during the years in which she was at work on the garden she published four full length novels, her collected poems and *Pepita*. In fact, as she wrote to H.N. one rainy day, she felt "how fortunate we both are to have both indoor and outdoor occupations. If we can't garden, we can write."[15]

In May 1930, V S-W published the first of these books. *The Edwardians*. This was, as Leonard Woolf remarked:

> a novel about Knole, the Sackvilles, and Edwardian Society with the most aristocratic capital S, written from the inside of not only Knole, but also Vita. Inside Vita was an honest, simple, sentimental, romantic, naïve, and competent writer. When she let all this go off altogether in a novel about high life, she produced in *The Edwardians* a kind of period piece and a real best-seller. . . . We sold nearly 30,000 copies of *The Edwardians* in the first six months, and by the end of the year the Press had made a profit of nearly £2,000 on it. It has gone on selling for years.[16]

Leonard Woolf's summary of the contents of the book is correct as far as it goes, but is far from adequate. For one thing, as S.P.B. Mais pointed out, "Quite apart from its interest as a human story, it is an historical document of great importance".[17] It describes "the Edwardians themselves, the very highest society, chiefly the fast set but also the intensely respectable set which was gradually even then decaying, though its power was still immense."[18]

It is not, however, a one-sided picture that V S-W presents. Her strong feeling for tradition and the consciousness of her aristocratic background on one hand and, on the other, the dislike she had felt for what she had regarded as the artificiality and uselessness of the society life her mother had indulged in, are here in conflict.

Sebastian states one side of the problem when he discusses the future of Chevron —Knole—and himself with his sister Viola:

> I will agree with you that Chevron, and myself, and Wickenden, and the whole apparatus are nothing but a waxwork show, if you like. Present-day conditions have made us all rather meaningless. But I still think that that is a pity. I think we had evolved a good system on the whole, which made for a good understanding between class and class. Nothing will ever persuade me that the relations between the squire and the craftsman, or the squire and the labourer, or the squire and the farmer, don't contain the elements of decency and honesty and mutual respect. I wish only that civilisation could have developed along these lines.[19]

The reverse side of the medal, the empty selfishness of the fast set, relieved only by their rigid adherence to a code of behaviour, has been mentioned previously (supra, p. 24.) Numerous instances are to be found in the book, such as when Viola enlightens a rather naïve young girl of her acquaintance as to the true nature of society:

> "Very well, if you want the truth, here it is. The society you live in is composed

---

[14] *Ibid.*, p. 268.
[15] *Ibid.*, p. 183.
[16] *Downhill all the Way*, p. 158.
[17] *Daily Telegraph*, May, 1930.
[18] *Times Literary Supplement,* 29 May, 1930, p. 454.
[19] *The Edwardians*, p. 182.

of people who are both dissolute and prudent. They want to have their fun, and they want to keep their position. They glitter on the surface, but underneath the surface they are stupid—too stupid to recognise their own motives. They know only a limited number of things about themselves: that they need plenty of money, and that they must be seen in the right places, associated with the right people. In spite of their efforts to turn themselves into painted images, they remain human somewhere, and must indulge in love-affairs, which sometimes are artificial, and sometimes inconveniently real. Whatever happens, this world must be served first. In spite of their brilliance, this creed necessarily makes them paltry and mean. Then they are envious, spiteful, and mercenary; arrogant and cold. As for us, their children, they leave us in complete ignorance of life, passing on to us only the ideas they think we should hold, and treat us with the utmost ruthlessness if we fail to conform."[20]

V S-W's concern with the good and evil sides of an oligarchical society seems quite understandable in view of her childhood experiences and her natural outlook. What perhaps strikes one as a little more surprising is the basically socialist solution which is here and there put forward, both in *The Edwardians,* and in *Family History,*[21] which deals to a great extent with the same question. It might not seem to be in keeping with the general tenor of V S-W's ideas. The explanation is quite possibly to be sought in the influence of Virginia and Leonard Woolf. The characters of Viola and Leonard Antequil, who figure in both these books, clearly owe a great deal to the Woolfs, who have obviously inspired them, and in both books it is Viola and Leonard, especially the former, who put forward the radical suggestions.

Finally, *The Edwardians* is partly biographical. The first two chapters in particular, describing Sebastian's childhood and the organisation and running of a great country house, give a detailed and probably highly accurate description of life at Knole as V S-W knew it in the first decade of this century.

"We published *The Edwardians* in 1930" writes Leonard Woolf, "and *All Passion Spent,* which she wrote in less than a year, in 1931. This was, I think, the best novel which she ever wrote, though there was rather more than a touch of sentimentality in it. It did very well, though not as well as *The Edwardians,* selling about 15,000 copies in the first year—it still sells 35 years after it was first published—and showing a profit of about £1,200."[22]

The subject of the novel has been variously described as "a study of extreme old age . . . the unsual feat is actually accomplished here of presenting old age as something worth creating in itself . . . and that period of life which new young writers have delighted to ransack for what they could despise is here made important without an evasion or exaggeration,"[23] and as "the study of a contemplative nature, of a woman with the sensibility and ambitions of an artist, caught up by her marriage into the life of a public man, Viceroy and Prime Minister, and left, an aged widow, to weigh her achievement and mould her last years to her own pattern."[24]

While both these descriptions are essentially correct, the second probably comes closer to the circumstances from which the idea of the novel sprang. The original conception of Deborah Slane, compelled to sacrifice her artistic aspirations on the altar of her husband's career, was almost certainly inspired by feelings V S-W must herself

[20] *Ibid.,* pp. 121—2.
[21] Hogarth Press, London, 1932.
[22] *Downhill all the Way,* p. 159.
[23] *New Statesman and Nation,* I (6 June, 1931), 547.
[24] *Manchester Guardian,* 2 June, 1931, p. 11.

have experienced a few years earlier, before H.N. had decided to leave the Diplomatic Corps and join the staff of the *Evening Standard*. Deborah Slane did what V S-W had refused to do, but she must at the time have considered the whole question of to what extent a woman was justified in sacrificing her own creative talents to her husband's career. The emancipation of women was still a question of current interest at that time, but V S-W was not a feminist in the ordinary sense of the word. Deborah's thoughts are probably to be interpreted as referring not so much to women in general as to V S-W in particular when she supposed that:

> even had she been in love with [Henry], she could see therein no reason for fore-going the whole of her own separate existence. Henry was in love with her, but no one proposed that he should forego his. On the contrary, it appeared that in acquiring her he was merely adding something extra to it. He would continue to lunch with his friends, travel down to his constituency, and spend his evenings at the House of Commons; he would continue to enjoy his free, varied, and masculine life, with no ring upon his finger or difference in his name to indicate the change in his estate; but whenever he felt inclined to come home she must be there, ready to lay down her book, her paper, or her letters; she must be prepared to listen to whatever he had to say; she must entertain his political acquaintances; and even if he beckoned her across the world she must follow. . . . But where, in such a programme, was there room for a studio?[25]

At least one of the grievances mentioned in this extract, the fact that a married woman has to adopt her husband's name for all official purposes, will be recognised as being one of the characteristic features of V S-W's nature that have already been discussed (supra, p. 46).

The year 1931 was also the year in which H.N. made his first, brief, appearance in politics—as a member of Sir Oswald Mosley's New Party and editor of its short-lived newspaper *Action*. V S-W thought the whole venture insane.[26]

Politics was the one field in which there was open disagreement between H.N. and V S-W. This is true both of 1931, and, even more, of 1935, when H.N. stood for election as National Labour candidate for West Leicester. He had hoped to enlist her active support during his election campaign, at least to the extent of her sitting on his platform once or twice during his speeches. However, V S-W refused pointblank to have anything to do with the electioneering. This led to a certain amount of accusation and recrimination, but it had all passed over before polling day, when H.N. was returned to Westminster. A brief account of this incident is to be found in H.N.'s diaries.[27]

It is quite possibly because of the unsuccessful venture of 1931 that politics creep into V S-W's novel *Family History*.[28] Miles Vane-Merrick, the brilliant young politician in the story, would appear to be a combination of the personality of H.N. and the political and economic theories of Maynard Keynes—also a sympathiser with Mosley's New Party for a short time—and his home in Kent bears a remarkable similarity to Sissinghurst Castle. One of the themes of the book—Evelyn's inability to comprehend, other than in an abstract manner, the importance to Miles of his political work[29]—may very well also have been inspired by the differences between V S-W and H.N. caused by almost exactly the same circumstances.

[25] *All Passion Spent*, pp. 160—1.
[26] *Diaries and Letters, 1930—39*, p. 67.
[27] *Ibid.*, pp. 218—25.
[28] Hogarth Press, London, 1932.
[29] *Family History*, pp. 144—50.

The main theme of the story is the love affair between two people from entirely different social backgrounds. Evelyn Jarrold comes from the Victorian middle class, and has married into a *nouveau riche* family of similar origins and outlook. Miles Vane-Merrick, on the other hand, is of the landed gentry; furthermore he is an intellectual who has espoused the cause of the Labour Party, which he represents in Parliament. Around this central situation V S-W has constructed a framework of social contrasts to illustrate her ideas. At one extreme there is the fast set of the aristocracy, here, as in *The Edwardians*, represented by Sebastian's mother and the Roehamptons. This enables V S-W to comment, through the mouth of Ruth Jarrold, on "the English upper classes (a horrid expression, but she must define them somehow)":[30]

> They looked as though for generations they had been well fed, well warmed, well exercised, and nourished in the conviction that the world could not produce their peers. The standard of looks was amazing; they had the distinction and beauty of thoroughbred animals. The young men were as elegant as greyhounds. the young women coloured as a herbaceous border. What did it matter, Ruth would have added, has she thought of it, that those sleek heads contained no more brains than a greyhound's, since those slender bodies expressed an equal grace? What did it matter that their code should strangely enough involve a contempt for the intellectual advantages which might have been theirs? What did it matter that they should immure themselves within the double barricade of their class and their nationality?[30]

At the other extreme is the middle-class morality of the Jarrolds, who "believe in reputation and in respectability and in keeping up appearances."[31] Here one must make an exception for old Mr Jarrold, who, despite his millions, remains at heart the unspoilt working-man he has always been.

Both extremes are equally sterile in their way. However, redemption is offered through the Antequils (here, as in *The Edwardians*, almost certainly based on the Woolfs) and through those intellectuals, such as Miles Vane-Merrick and Dan, the young heir to the Jarrold empire, who have been influenced by the Antequils' outlook on life.

Although the book has sterling qualities—"She begins with a splendid Thackerayan description of her chief people; she ends with a poignantly tragic account of Evelyn's death"[32]—there is a great deal of truth in the criticism that "there are moments when *Family History* threatens to become less a novel than a tract. Its interest is almost equally divided between the romance and the thesis, and, unfortunately, there is no very strong or necessary connection between the two. For Evelyn Jarrold and her lover are separated, in the end, more by reason of the disparity of their ages than of their backgrounds and ideals."[33] The inappositeness of the title excited comment in several reviews.[34]

V S-W published one other book in 1932, a collection of short-stories entitled *Thirty Clocks Strike the Hour*.[35] Except for the title story, "The Poet", and "Pomodoro", all

[30] *Ibid.,* p. 53.
[31] *Ibid.,* p. 141.
[32] *New Statesman and Nation,* IV (22 October, 1932), 490.
[33] *New York Times,* Book Review, 30 October, 1932, p. 7.
[34] *Times Literary Supplement,* 13 October, 1932, p. 730; *Manchester Guardian,* 28 October, 1932; *Saturday Review of Literature,* 31 December, 1932, p. 353.
[35] Doubleday, Doran, New York, 1932. In England, two only of the stories, "The Death of Noble Godavary" and "Gottfried Künstler", were published by Benn, London, in 1932 under the title *The Death of Noble Godavary.*

the stories in the volume had already been published separately in various magazines in Great Britain.[36]

The story entitled "The Poet" is interesting for the light it casts upon one aspect of the relationship between V S-W and her poetry. The story is about a consumptive young poet, living in Italy, who tells a compatriot he has met there that he is convinced that some, at least, of the poetry he has hammered out with such care is truly great, and will one day make his name immortal. When, after the poet's death a few weeks later, the Englishman goes through his papers in order to rescue these masterpieces for posterity, he finds that the poems really are of the highest quality, as the poet had told him that they were. What he has arrived at, after endless trial and error, are almost word for word copies of some of the most famous poems in the English language.

The inspiration for this story is almost certainly to be found in an experience V S-W had had. Twelve years after the publication of "The Poet", H.N. had occasion to mention to V S-W that the poet Edward Shanks, with whom he had recently had a conversation, complained that he was unable to remember whether a line of poetry was one of his own, or something that he had read years before. To this V S-W replied:

> As to remembering whether a line is by me or by someone else, you know very well that I never could. The first shock of this realisation came when I very laboriously hammered out a line, choosing every word most carefully, and arrived at:
>
> 'Men are but children of a larger growth.'
>
> Since then I have been cautious.[37]

In itself, this is perhaps not so remarkable; other poets besides Shanks and V S-W have probably had similar experiences. There is, however, an interesting sequel.

In the summer of 1949, the *Poetry Review* asked V S-W if she could let them have some unpublished verses for their jubilee number. She looked through her MSS Book and sent them a poem entitled "The Novice to her Lover", which she had written in late 1942 or early 1943. Shortly after the poem had appeared in 1949, V S-W discovered that Clifford Dyment had published an almost identical poem entitled "Saint Augustine at 32" in 1943 and had later reprinted it in a book of collected poems. The discovery led to an interesting exchange of letters which was published in the *New Statesman and Nation*.[38] V S-W considers it "unthinkable that either I or Mr. Dyment should have 'lifted' a poem from one another. That supposition can be dismissed." So, of course, it can, if by "lifted" she means "consciously lifted". In view of the remarkable resemblance, both in words and in metre, that the two poems bear to one another, and in view of V S-W's avowed inability to remember what lines are hers and what lines were written by somebody else, there can hardly be much doubt that, subconsciously, she had been strongly influenced by a memory of the poem which she had probably read in the *St. Martin's Review* in January 1943.

The first three months of 1933 saw H.N. and V S-W on a lecture tour of the United States. They lectured, separately and together, all over the country and the tour was, by all accounts, extremely successful.[39] How V S-W herself experienced the tour is shown in a letter she wrote to H.N.:

[36] See infra, p. 122.
[37] *Diaries and Letters, 1939—45*, pp. 447—8.
[38] *New Statesman and Nation*, 21 January, 1950, p. 62. A copy of the article will be found in Appendix B, on pp. 111—3.
[39] *Diaries and Letters, 1930—39*, pp. 129—30.

I think it is very good for you and me to have to come to America. I am glad we did. I am getting a lot out of it. There may be moments when we are tired and nauseated and bored. But on the whole it is infinitely valuable.[40]

If this is not enthusiastic, it is at least positive. Indeed, she never seems to have been as averse to America and Americans as H.N. obviously was.[41] The more spectacular scenery, such as the Niagara Falls and the Grand Canyon, made a great impression on her, but she found that "with all their kindness, these people have very little imagination".[42] The cities, in particular, filled her with dismay:

> Earth and not pavement lay beneath my feet;
> The anger of a dozen rushing brooks
> Replaced the clamour of a city street
> And vapid endless talk of books, books, books.[43]

The immediate literary results of V S-W's visit to the United States were three poems published in her *Collected Poems* the same autumn, as well as one which she never published.[44] Nine years later she was to write *Grand Canyon*.[45] The view of America that she gives in this book corresponds, by and large, to the one she appears to have held in 1933, except that the portrayal of an average American family is presented in a less flattering light than one would have expected.

> The Driscolls' house resembles all the other houses set along that road. They would not like it to differ in any way. They have lived in it for thirty years and are satisfied with it, though I would not say that they have ever thought of it otherwise than as a convenient and suitable residence. It stands exposed to the glances of passers-by on the road, and to the gaze of the neighbours on either side, but it has never occurred to the Driscolls any more than it has ever occurred to anyone else in the village that privacy might be secured by the planting of a hedge or the erection of a fence. Such things are not done, nor have the Driscolls any wish to do them. Life is pure and open and democratic, so pure as to be almost meaningless, so democratic as to be almost communal. ... Mr Driscoll is ... obviously a man of the utmost rectitude and probity. In business, of course, he would not hesitate to get the better of a weaker rival, would not hesitate to take advantage of someone else's mistake, but in no way would he consider this a departure from the high moral standard of his private life. Possibly this is because he has never thought about it; possibly because in business, as in private life, he accepts other people's standards as he finds them, ready made.[46]

Collected Poems appeared in late 1933. Besides *The Land, Sissinghurst,* and many of the poems which had been published in *Constantinople, Poems of West and East, Orchard and Vineyard* and *King's Daughter,* it contained 23 poems previously published only in newspapers or periodicals, and 35 poems that had not been printed before at all.

The appearance of a volume of poems with this title naturally led some critics to sum up V S-W's position in poetry. One commented that "this collection of poems has

[40] *Ibid.,* p. 136.
[41] *Ibid.,* pp. 24—5.
[42] *Ibid.,* p. 136.
[43] "In New England", *Collected Poems,* London, 1933, p. 212.
[44] "Minnesota", MS at Sissinghurst Castle.
[45] Michael Joseph, London, 1942.
[46] *Grand Canyon,* pp. 20—1. The book is also discussed on pp. 65, 86 infra.

a double interest: first, its beauty, and, secondly, its historical position. Unified and complete, it stands like a frontier tower on the border of a land that we are leaving behind. That land is the England which is vanishing; the England of a ripe and comely rural civilisation which has been sung by Crabbe, Cowper, Thomson, Gray, Tennyson, Hardy, Bridges, and Blunden."[47] The poetry in the volume is discussed elsewhere.

Early in 1934, in January, V S-W and Gwen St. Aubyn, H.N.'s sister, went to Portofino, where they took a short lease of the Castello, overlooking the harbour.[48] In February, accompanied this time by H.N., they went to Morocco for a month before returning to Sissinghurst. In the autumn, V S-W published *The Dark Island*,[49] dedicated to Gwen St. Aubyn.

Of all V S-W's books, none has been received with such wide differences of opinion as this. The *Times Literary Supplement* wrote:

> *The Dark Island*, a work of fervid and disciplined imagination, is concerned chiefly with the life of Shirin le Breton, a woman who becomes real to us almost by the very improbabilities of her character, or by the way in which the author, forcing us to assume her premises, convinces us of her conclusions. . . . This would be a moving and very exciting story in any hands, but it takes the skill of an accomplished writer to make it a work of art as well.[50]

The *New York Times* was equally positive,[51] as was the *Manchester Guardian*.[52] The *New Statesman and Nation* admitted that the book had great merits, but added "if only Miss Sackville-West had refused all compromise with a superficial plausibility it might have had in it something of greatness."[53] Leonard Woolf had "grave doubts . . . about *The Dark Island*,"[54] and H.N. wrote in a letter to V S-W:

> Darling, I am sorry I don't like *The Dark Island*. But then if I just said I liked all your books, it would detract from the ones I do like. I think I like *Sissinghurst* the best of anything you have ever written—but that may be personal. But I think nonetheless that it *is* the best you have ever written. Then *The Land*. Then *Knole*. Then Lady Anne [*The Diary of Lady Anne Clifford*]. Then Marvell. Then *Challenge*. Then *Heritage*. Then Dragon [*The Dragon in Shallow Waters*]. Then G.W. [*Grey Wethers*]. Then *The Heir*. Then King's Daughter. Then A.P.S. [*All Passion Spent*]. Then *The Edwardians*. . . . thenthedarkisland. I cannot judge of the two Persian books since they mean so much to me, but I think I should put them after Lady Anne. I think I should put *Family History* after the Dragon. Thus you see, I put *The Edwardians* and this book last on the list.[55]

Two interrelated aspects of V S-W's character are illustrated more clearly in *The Dark Island* than in any other of her books—her arrogance, and the streak of cruelty that one had already guessed at in *The Dragon in Shallow Waters* and other books. These two traits are especially noticeable in the manner in which the character of Venn is handled. It is the atmosphere created in the description of several incidents which shows that these traits are not merely reflections of tendencies inherent in the characters portrayed. As examples may be taken Venn's arrogant treatment of his grandmother,

[47] Richard Church in the *New Statesman & Nation*, VII (12 May, 1934), 740.
[48] *Diaries and Letters, 1930—39*, p. 163.
[49] Hogarth Press, London, 1934.
[50] *Times Literary Supplement*, 11 October, 1934, p. 692.
[51] *Book Review*, 25 November, 1934, p. 6.
[52] 2 November, 1934.
[53] VIII (1 December, 1934), 794.
[54] *Downhill All the Way*, p. 159.
[55] *Diaries and Letters, 1930—39*, pp. 185—6.

his acquaintances, and above all, of Shirin, when he discovers that it is Storn she loves, not him[56], and the cruelty of the unpleasant, sadistic little incident when he whips the naked Shirin in Andromeda's Cave.[57].

Leonard Woolf, an acute observer of such characteristics, comments:

> To be driven by Vita on a summer's afternoon at the height of the season through the London traffic—she was a very good, but rather flamboyant driver—and to hear her put an aggressive taxi driver in his place, even when she was in the wrong, made one recognize a note in her voice that Sackvilles and Buckhursts were using to serfs in Kent 600 years ago, or even in Normandy 300 years before that. She belonged indeed to a world which was completely different from ours, and the long line of Sackvilles, Dorsets, De La Warrs, and Knole with its 365 rooms had put into her mind and heart an ingredient which was alien to us and at first made intimacy difficult.[58]

Later, when he had got to know V S-W better, he wrote:

> Vita was in many ways an extremely unassuming and modest person, but below the surface, and not so very much below, she had the instinctive arrogance of the aristocrat of the ancient regime, and above the surface she was keenly conscious of the long line of her ancestors, the Sackvilles, Buckhursts, and Dorsets, and of the great house of Knole a few miles away in Kent.[59]

The Dark Island is, to some extent at least, a *roman à clef*. Shirin is a slightly romanticised version of Gwen St. Aubyn (later Lady St. Levan), to whom the book is dedicated,[60] and Cristina represents V S-W herself. Storn, the dark island, is directly modelled on the St. Levans' home, St. Michael's Mount in Cornwall.[61] On the other hand, Venn is not a portrait of Lord St. Levan, "who is quite a different sort of man" according to Mr Nigel Nicolson.

There are probably two or three different reasons which would explain the dislike that some people took to *The Dark Island,* which is in fact a powerful, well-written novel. A few, like Leonard Woolf, would have detected the streak of arrogance and cruelty in the book and been disturbed by it. H.N., one of the severest critics of the novel, must have recognised in Shirin a portrait of his sister, Gwen St. Aubyn, and in Cristina, his wife, and taken a dislike to the book for personal reasons. Others, as the reviewer writing in the *Manchester Guardian,* evidently understood, would have found the story rather strong meat, for she plainly states:

> Do not read Miss Sackville-West's novel unless you are strong enough; it will be rather like throwing your hat into the lion's den. But if after this warning you can protect yourself and go armed, your reward will be a feast of fire and beauty.[62]

Unlike the three previous novels, *The Edwardians, All Passion Spent* and *Family History, The Dark Island* does not appear to be a straightforward tale. The observant reader will probably become aware that the book has a secret quality, that there are currents running below the surface of the story which may disturb or excite him according to his nature. This quality is less obvious in *The Dark Island* than in *Seducers in Ecuador,* but one or two reviews contain sentences which seem to indicate that their authors are conscious of hidden depths: "The dream island of Storn . . . is one of those

---

[56] *The Dark Island*, pp. 48, 139, 179.
[57] *Ibid.,* pp. 59, 255—6.
[58] *Downhill all the Way,* p. 112.
[59] *The Journey not the Arrival Matters,* Hogarth Press, London, 1969, p. 57.
[60] This was confirmed by Mr Nigel Nicolson in a letter of 13 January, 1971.
[61] The name "Storn" was possibly suggested to V S-W by the name of Lord Beaverbrook's home, Stornoway House, which H.N. had recently visited several times.
[62] *Manchester Guardian,* 2 November, 1934, p. 11.

dark inheritances of an ancient line, to the governance of which its heads are ineluctably devoted from the moment of their conception"[63] is one reviewer's comment. "Poets sometimes mix symbols and personalities together and forget which is which"[64] is another. The very mixed reception that the book met with was probably connected with considerations similar to those above.

1935 was a rather uneventful year for V S-W. H.N. was in America during the first part of the year to continue work on the biography of Dwight Morrow that he had begun the previous autumn. In April he was back in Europe and he, V S-W and Nigel Nicolson went on a cruise to Greece. In January 1936, Lady Sackville died at Brighton.[65] One consequence of her death was that the terms of her will brought the Nicolsons financial security and independence for the first time since their marriage, as she left V S-W a considerable sum of money. Up to this time they had, as Mr Nigel Nicolson points out,[66] been living a very hand to mouth existence and had taken a good few financial risks.

In the autumn of 1935, V S-W had started work on her next book, which was to be a study of the life of Jeanne d'Arc. *Saint Joan of Arc*[67] proved to be a biography on a very different scale from V S-W's two previous essays in this genre; in neither of those works had she penetrated so deeply into the subject of the biography as she did in the life of Jeanne d'Arc. This is possibly because her reasons for choosing Mrs Behn and Marvell to write about were of a less urgent nature; her main interest in them appears to have been certain aspects of their writing.[68] Her choice of Jeanne d'Arc, on the other hand, was probably motivated by a far deeper emotion; by the need to examine her own attitude to religion, and to clarify her mind on certain religious questions. The book entailed a good deal of reading, research and thought on her part, and in October 1935 it had taken her, accompanied by Gwen St. Aubyn, to Domrémy, Chinon and Orleans. The resulting work was, in the words of one critic, "a new interpretation". He added:

> Patience, intuition and wide reading have made her completely at home. ... It appears that she has deliberately set herself to avoid emotion and to write in a sober, even at times a pedestrian, strain. The effect is at first a little disappointing, but as we settle down to a book which it is very difficult to stop reading we appreciate more and more the biographer's method. Not only are the events narrated with admirable clarity; the portrait that emerges is as impressive as it is satisfactory and the speculation intelligent, if cautious. Caution itself is a merit here; and one is indeed grateful to Miss Sackville-West for not proclaiming that she is the inspired solver of the great mystery.[69]

One of the results of choosing Jeanne d'Arc as the subject of her biography was that it forced V S-W to think clearly about and to try to come to some definite conclusion on certain aspects of religion. Indeed, this may well have been the main reason why she chose to write the biography of a saint at all, and Saint Joan in particular, she being the most relevant for the problems V S-W had on her mind.

As we shall see, there is clear evidence that during the years from 1936 to 1945

---

[63] *New Statesman and Nation,* VIII (1 December, 1934), 794.
[64] *Manchester Guardian,* 2 November, 1934, p. 11.
[65] *Diaries and Letters, 1930—39,* p. 241.
[66] *Ibid.,* p. 28.
[67] Cobden, Sanderson, London, 1936. In this dissertation, the edition by Penguin Books, London, 1955, has been used throughout.
[68] See also infra, pp. 93, 97.
[69] *Times Literary Supplement,* 6 June, 1936, p. 469.

V S-W was much concerned with religious questions, to which she was endeavouring to find an answer which would have meaning for her personally. The volume of poetry she published in 1938, *Solitude*,[70] has as its central themes death and religion (infra, p. 67), motifs that are also noticeable in *The Garden*.[71] In 1943 she published *The Eagle and the Dove*,[72] comparing the lives of two saints very different from each other in every way: Saint Teresa of Avila, and Saint Thérèse of Lisieux. In *Saint Joan of Arc* it is the question of miracles and other supernatural phenomena on which she has to make up her mind.

She defines herself as being:

not what is called a 'religious' person in the orthodox sense of the phrase, nor yet a practising member of any organized Church. I do, however, confronted with the ultimate enigma, believe, and believe deeply, in some mysterious central originating force which the natural weakness and insufficiency of human nature finds it necessary to symbolize in a name, an amalgam of fear and comfort, which you may call God or Gott or Dieu or Jah or Allah or X, or even 'a pure mathematician', without any reason *necessarily* to identify that force with our own human conceptions of good and evil. It follows logically that, holding this belief, I share with my fellow-mortals the ancient superstition which no scientific explanation can destroy, but which no scientific explanation has as yet been able to account for: the belief in what we conveniently call the supernatural. I believe in it so profoundly as to quarrel with the expressions supernatural or extra-natural. For me there is only one comprehensive, stupendous unity of which we apprehend but the smallest segment.[73]

For many of Jeanne d'Arc's miracles, for example the famous 'King's secret', and her ability to pick out the disguised Dauphin from among his courtiers, V S-W attempts to find a natural explanation. In those cases where she is unable to find one that satisfies her, Jeanne's "Voices" for example, she confesses she is "in the unfortunate position of anybody torn between an instinctive reliance on instinct, and a reasonable reliance on reason."[74] She determines to keep an open mind about them in the belief that the future may be able to provide a scientific explanation to what, at present, must be taken on faith.

During the early months of 1937 both the Nicolsons were away, H. N. on a Government Commission to the African colonies to report on education,[75] and V S-W, with Gwen St. Aubyn, on a tour of Algeria and Morocco.[76] They all returned to Sissinghurst in March, when V S-W settled down to write *Pepita*. Sufficient has already been said in this work about the contents; from the critics' point of view it was probably the most successful of her books, the response being almost universally positive. The fantastic nature of this true story fascinated them, and they particularly praised V S-W for the "great candour, great understanding and great love"[77] with which she had described her mother, of whom she "has drawn an enduring portrait, firm in its lines, but profuse

---

[70] Hogarth Press, London.
[71] Michael Joseph, London, 1946.
[72] Michael Joseph, London. In this dissertation, the Mermaid Book edition, Michael Joseph, London, 1953, has been used throughout.
[73] *Saint Joan of Arc*, p. 382.
[74] *Ibid.*, p. 383.
[75] *Diaries and Letters, 1930—39*, p. 291.
[76] *Ibid.*, p. 295.
[77] *New Statesman and Nation*, XIV (30 October, 1937), 695.

in detail of exquisite comedy, hiding little but explaining much."[78] There were a few acute critics, notably A.G. Macdonell in the *Observer*[79] and R.M. in the *New Statesman and Nation,*[77] who surmised that Lady Sackville must have been a far more distressing mother than the book suggested.

During the years between 1934 and 1947 V S-W did not produce much fiction. In Leonard Woolf's opinion, "the springs of Vita's invention and imagination which she required for novel writing began to run dry." He had had grave doubts about *Family History* and *The Dark Island,* and after *Pepita:*

> she brought us the manuscript of a novel which we felt we could not publish. . . . Vita was an ideal author from the publisher's point of view; she never complained when things went wrong and was extraordinarily appreciative of the publisher if they went right. This made it all the more unpleasant to have to tell her that we thought her novel not good enough for us to publish. We knew, too, that we should lose her as an author, because there were many reputable publishers who would publish this novel in order to get her 'on their list'.[80]

The novel was *Grand Canyon,*[81] which Michael Joseph published in November 1942. Interior evidence shows that the book must have been written after the fall of France in 1940, and if V S-W followed her normal practice, it was written in the twelve months preceding its publication, that is to say not long after Virginia Woolf had committed suicide in March 1941. V S-W was feeling rather depressed at the time,[82] and Virginia Woolf's death was naturally a great shock to her. Whatever the reason, *Grand Canyon* was not by any means up to her accustomed standard. It was variously said to "suffer from incredibility"[83] and, less bluntly, to be a "somewhat rarified story", which, half-way through, "takes a plunge into the symbolical".[84] It is here, perhaps, that one of the main sources of weakness lies, for although a number of features in the book are quite clearly symbols, they fail to mean what they ought, and their true significance never becomes apparent.

Leonard Woolf was quite right when he surmised that V S-W's books would no longer be published by the Hogarth Press. She had begun by publishing her poetry with John Lane, The Bodley Head, and her fiction with Collins until she had transferred to Heinemann's in 1922. Virginia Woolf had recruited her for the Hogarth Press in 1924 and, apart from *The Land,* which she had probably already promised to Heinemann's, and a few minor works, she had remained with the Hogarth Press until Virginia Woolf's death. Michael Joseph, to whom V S-W then transferred, was her publisher until her own death in 1962.

From 1937 until the end of the period covered by this chapter, that is up to the end of 1946, V S-W's life seems to have been outwardly uneventful. Immediately after the publication of *Pepita,* she and Gwen St. Aubyn spent some weeks in the south of France, and it was during this time that she conceived the idea of writing *The Eagle and the Dove* and *Solitude.*[85] Apart from this, she went abroad little more before the outbreak of war.

[78] *Times Literary Supplement,* 30 Oct., 1937, p. 796.
[79] 7 November, 1937, p. 11.
[80] *Downhill all the Way,* pp. 159—60.
[81] Letter dated 1/1/71 from Mr Nigel Nicolson to the present author.
[82] *Diaries and Letters, 1939—45,* pp. 156—7.
[83] *Observer,* 8 November, 1942, p. 3.
[84] *Times Literary Supplement,* 7 Nov. 1942, p. 545.
[85] *Diaries and Letters, 1930—39,* p. 311.

H.N. was fully occupied by politics during these years; it was with the deterioration of the international situation that his knowledge of foreign affairs proved an asset to the House of Commons.[86] He was in London for the greater part of every week, returning to Sissinghurst only at week-ends, and not always then. V S-W, on the other hand, spent most of her time in Kent.[87]

Inwardly, however, it would seem that these years were, for V S-W, not so calm and uneventful as they might have appeared on the surface. *Solitude,* the poem she published in 1938, is filled with signs of spiritual unrest. The introductory poem, "Rocamadour", dedicated to Gwen St. Aubyn, states:

> So, rightly, you divined
> That I within the trouble of my mind
> Would in Rocamadour a refuge find.
> . . .
> How did you know that I was worldly-sick?
> Because you knew, I dedicate this verse
> To you for better or for worse.[88]

The poem itself moves from the initial apparent optimism of:

> — but who would sleep when he might wake? . . .
> Wring the last midnight minute to its end?[89]

—an optimism that has a slight feeling of defiance about it—to the deeply pessimistic

> —but who would wake when he might sleep?
> Who live, when he might die? . . .
> Who would not rather, in this world of sin,
> Sleep in forgetfulness? choose sleep and death[90]

Leading up to this conclusion, V S-W gives a brief summary of the experiences of the spirit, of moods and outlooks, of "this tender hell of passion, love, tradition, closing jaws", of days when one was "dull, muted, sealed", of other days filled with happiness, "What gaiety, what joy, what faith extreme".

But at her back she always hears a whisper that urges:

> "Hurry on!
> "No time for admiration of the swan,
> "No time for balance and comparison,
> "Time only for the scrambling jettison
> "To save a labouring ship.
> "The port is Death; oh, hurry, hurry on!"[91]

Faced with the thought of death, with the necessity of yielding her further keeping "into such hands as planned this intricate I" she feels obliged to add:

> And since I know not what those hands may be
> I ask not whence? nor whether? nor yet why?
> I only know, not sadly, but resigned,

[86] *Diaries and Letters, 1939—45,* pp. 17—8.
[87] *Diaries and Letters, 1930—39,* p. 387.
[88] *Solitude,* p. 5.
[89] *Ibid.,* p. 7.
[90] *Ibid.,* p. 56.
[91] *Ibid.,* p. 37.

That in the humour of a master-mind
This name, this I, this label must be torn,
Scrapped with the implications that were me.[92]

It is true she says she is resigned to her fate. Furthermore, she goes on to say that she scorns religious consolation, and boasts:

No Church I need; I seek my God direct,
Knowing myself unchosen, unelect[93]

but, in reality, this is a pose, a device to bolster up her morale by pretending to a courage that she does not actually possess. At heart she is appalled, and feels the need of reassurance. She cries:

Give us a sign. Regard, O God, our need.
Give us a sign. We die without your heed.[94]

There comes no sign:

But silence meets me; all my prayer is vain.[95]

The dilemma for her is that she is unable to find by ratiocination any answer to the problems that beset her, and incapable by nature of accepting the answer which satisfies:

. . . that happy, enviable soul
Greeting the great solution of our doubt
Simply, to take it all-embracing, whole,
A charmèd circle, leaving us without.[96]

Hence the tragic feelings with which the poem ends.

There is one point of particular interest in the poem. When asking God for a sign to be given, V S-W singles out one aspect of her doubts as being of central significance, the key to all the problems confronting her, and puts it in the form of a concrete question, which it might be illuminating to consider:

We only ask to learn if you will teach
Class by enormous class, or each by each[97]

The most obvious interpretation of the question is that it asks whether knowledge of God's purpose will be revealed through the Church, or by individual enlightenment. If this is indeed what it means, it gives us a clear indication of the reason why V S-W was interested in hagiology in general, and in Jeanne d'Arc in particular. It was Jeanne's locutions that attracted her; were they indeed of God, or did they admit of some more mundane explanation?

If V S-W's interest in Jeanne d'Arc was primarily because she felt the need to form some opinion of the nature of Jeanne's locutions, it seems very likely that one of the reasons for her interest in Saint Teresa of Avila was that, as regards background, temperament, and some other features, she and Saint Teresa appeared to have a great deal in common.

Teresa de Cepeda Dávila y Ahumada, one of the subjects of *The Eagle and the Dove*, was of noble birth. She had received an ordinary aristocratic upbringing and had never,

[92] *Ibid.*, p. 20.
[93] *Ibid.*, p. 21.
[94] *Ibid.*, p. 46.
[95] *Ibid.*, p. 51.
[96] *Ibid.*, p. 48.
[97] *Ibid.*, p. 46.

as a child, had the least thought of devoting herself to the religious life. Her entry, as a pupil, not as a postulant, into the convent of Santa Maria de Gracia at the age of sixteen was imposed upon her from the outside; apparently the result of the discovery of a Lesbian relationship between her, a cousin and another girl.[98] Although originally hostile to the idea of becoming a nun; "estaba enemigisma de ser monja",[99] feelings of guilt and a fear of Hell persuaded her to enter a convent and eventually to take the veil. It was not until thirty years later, when she was in her fifties, that she began what was her real life work; the reformation of the Carmelite order in Spain.

She was a woman of immense practical common sense and strength of character, "one of the most capable women the world has seen",[100] as indeed she needed to be to deal with "shrewd men, suspicious prelates, and jealous organisations". "And", adds V S-W, "the reader who chooses to pick his way through the tangle recorded in the documents is left wondering not only at the dissentions and treacheries of the men of God but also at the stature of the woman steering amongst them".[101] But Saint Teresa was much more than an able administrator; she was a writer and, above all, a mystic. V S-W appreciated the writer for her clear, energetic, even homely prose, but also for the fact that "in addition to this factual, often of-the-soil vividness of expression, she possessed also something of the poet's vision, when her imagery flamed more splendid.";[102] it is, however, Saint Teresa the mystic who is the focus of V S-W's interest.

The mystic and the poet have much in common. In the first place, both are faced with the problem, even more difficult for the mystic'than the poet, of explaining their visions in ordinary language:

> The mystics themselves have dwelt on the hopelessness of the attempt to translate their experiences into intelligible words. Like the poet, they must take refuge in symbol and metaphor, more potent than dry affirmation, more evocative than statement.[103]

Secondly, and this is perhaps the essential feature for V S-W, there is the question of inspiration and vision. "We may well believe that the condition of the artist in moments of creative inspiration, the 'fine frenzy', is closely comparable to the rapture of the mystic; that the two experiences, in fact, are similar in their nature though perhaps not consciously in their aim."[104] Later she expands this statement, adding:

> for there is a greater resemblance between the creative artist and the mystic than between any other brands of human beings ... that sense of being lifted out of self, exalted, filled with power, filled with a perception not blinding but revealing —it must never be forgotten that the aim is not consciously similar, not similar even in retrospect; unless, indeed, the pursuit of beauty runs a parallel path to the pursuit of God. As well it may.[105]

While it is not difficult to see what it was that attracted V S-W's interest to Saint Teresa of Avila, it does not at first seem quite so clear what there was about Saint Thérèse of Lisieux that made V S-W choose her as the second saint for this "Study in Contrasts", as the subtitle of the book calls it. The idea of writing *The Eagle and the Dove* first came to V S-W in 1937, while she and her sister-in-law, Gwen St. Aubyn, were motoring through the south of France. V S-W evidently told H.N. of her inten-

[98] *The Eagle and the Dove,* p. 28.
[99] *Ibid.,* p. 30.
[100] *Ibid.,* p. 68.
[101] *Ibid.,* p. 69.
[102] *Ibid.,* p. 60.
[103] *Ibid.,* p. 44.
[104] *Ibid.,* pp. 43—4.
[105] *Ibid.,* p. 146.

tion, for in October he wrote to her mentioning St. Thérèse of Lisieux. This letter has been printed in *Diaries and Letters, 1930—39*[106] with the addition of a footnote stating that "V. S-W had just conceived the idea of writing *The Eagle and the Dove.*" Although the idea came to her then, it seems that she did not actually write the book until several years later, for the "acknowledgements" mention the fact that it was written "under war-time conditions".[107]

Further enlightenment is provided by an article written in 1950 about one of V S-W's poems.[108] In this article, V S-W states that "I wrote my poem *The Novice to her Lover* some time in 1942 or early in 1943, when I was engaged on an essay about St. Thérèse of Lisieux, the 'novice' and I had in mind." She sent the poem to "a recently converted Catholic and a devotee of St. Thérèse . . . embodied in a letter."[109] It seems almost certain that the person referred to was Gwen St. Aubyn. The latter was a convert and lived nearby in a house in Sissinghurst village during the early years of the war.[110] It therefore seems likely that V S-W's interest in St. Thérèse was aroused by her sister-in-law and that, contrary to what might have been supposed, it was with this saint that V S-W was originally concerned, St. Teresa of Avila, with whom she would have been far more in sympathy, being added later.

There can be little doubt that there were problems of a religious nature on V S-W's mind about this time. After the publication of *The Eagle and the Dove* there was a widespread rumour that she was about to become a Roman Catholic. She denied it.[111] One cannot, however, escape being aware of the fact that she had devoted very serious thought to the question. *Saint Joan of Arc,* 1936, *Solitude,* 1938, and *The Eagle and the Dove,* 1943, show a progressively deeper concern for and a greater knowledge of religious, especially Catholic, problems. The last of these books in particular could not have been written without undertaking a considerable amount of study of the dogma of the Church. Though by no means uncritical of certain aspects of Catholicism, such as the question of relics, the underlying tone of the book as a whole bespeaks a basic acceptance of the spirit of the Roman Catholic Church which indicates that the writer is, to say the least, positively disposed towards it:

> The roaring of the crowd was silenced only by the command to stand while Peter should speak through the lips of Pius. Strange, awesome ritual of this Church with all its hierarchy, tradition, power, splendour and organisation, so self-contained within the framework of the temporal realms of this world, so immutable, so secret in its workings among the hearts of millions, so apparent in its majesty on such occasions of affirmation in its Roman stronghold![112]

As we saw in *Solitude,* V S-W seems to have had a strong desire to be able to believe, and envied those who were capable, by a simple act of faith, of cutting straight through to the heart of those questions which were problems to her. *Solitude* also indicates that she thought that there were two possible paths which might lead her to belief: the teaching of the Church, on one hand, and revelation on the other. She had studied the revelations of one saint and the mysticism of two others, presumably in order to find out what she could learn from their experiences. It is, of course, not possible to come to

---

[106] P. 311.
[107] *The Eagle and the Dove,* p. 7.
[108] "Question of Inspiration", *New Statesman and Nation,* 21 January, 1950, p. 62. The article is reprinted in Appendix B infra.
[109] *Loc. cit.*
[110] Letter dated 28/4/69 from Mr Nigel Nicolson to the present author.
[111] *Diaries and Letters, 1939—45,* p. 333.
[112] *The Eagle and the Dove,* p. 183.

any conclusion about what she decided in her own mind, but it is clear that several years of speculation and study had brought her to a position in which the Catholic Church exercised a certain attraction on her. It would have been reasonable to expect her to continue to study Catholicism and to deepen her knowledge of the Church still further, in which case probably no one would have been surprised if she had eventually been received into the Roman Catholic Church. But she does not. Problems of religious belief still beset her, as witness *The Garden,* but she no longer seeks an answer by turning to the lives of the saints, or considering the doctrines of Rome. Instead, a pantheistic outlook appears in her work. A short poem probably written about this time is entitled "Litany: I am"[113]

> I am the snail crawling out at night to devour the flower.
> I am the flower devoured by the snail—
> I am the lion in his desert
> I am the gazelle brought down by the lion—
> I am the dog who lies down by man's hearth.
> I am the horse—who was once no bigger than a hare but who
>   now pulls men's carriages and farm-waggons.
> I have grown to the Suffolk Punch and the Percheron—
> I am the man
> I am the star—the black dwarf
> I am the Galaxy
> I am the speed of light
> I am the atom. I am the atom bomb.
> I am the Universe, receding so fast that no telescope can
>   catch up with it.
> I AM, because I think I am.[114]

The Garden, which contains a variation on this theme,[115] is an introspective poem, the inner motif of which is a reflection on the conflicting aspects of Christianity and pantheism. The tendency is to reject the former in favour of the latter.[116] The same conflict is, as we shall see,[117] one of the themes of *The Easter Party,*[118] although the conclusions reached there appear to be a little different.

The exact reason for this sudden and rather surprising change of attitude must, of course, remain a matter for conjecture. There are, however, good grounds for believing that is was due to the break-up of a personal relationship with a close friend due to the latter's religious convictions, as the following lines from a poem entitled "Requiem" seem to show:

> I had not thought that you who shared
> My days, my nights, my heart, my life,
> Would slash me with a naked knife
> And gently tell me not to bleed
> But to accept your crazy creed.

---

[113] Unpublished poem. The MS is in the possession of Mr Nigel Nicolson.
[114] There is a remarkable similarity between this poem and another, by Amergin, entitled "Song of Triumph" to be found in *Bards of the Gael and Gall,* ed. George Sigerson, London, 1907, pp. 110—1.
[115] *The Garden,* pp. 70—1.
[116] Stevens, "An Analysis of *The Garden*", p. 48. (Unpublished thesis, Uppsala University.)
[117] See infra, pp. 76—7 & 85—6.
[118] Michael Joseph, London, 1953. In this dissertation the Mermaid Books edition, Michael Joseph, 1955, is used throughout.

You speak of God, but you have cut
The one last thread, as you have shut
The one last door that open stood
To show me still the way to God.
If this be God, this pain, this evil,
I'd sooner change and try the Devil.

. . .

But tell me once before I cease,
Which does your Church esteem the kinder role,
To kill the body, or destroy the soul?[119]

The manuscript is undated, but was found by the present author in December 1963, lying last in a file marked "Mostly 1940 to 1945". The file had almost certainly not been looked at since V S-W's death. If it was written sometimes between the publishing of *The Eagle and the Dove,* in the autumn of 1943, and the time when the relevant passages of *The Garden* were written, in late 1944, it may well be the explanation of V S-W's sudden loss of interest in Catholicism. It is worth noting also that *The Garden* is a poem with an underlying tone of deep pessimism, and is filled with clear signs of spiritual unrest.[120] The balance and harmony which characterized *The Eagle and the Dove* are lacking.

The publication of *The Garden* marked the end of a period in V S-W's life and authorship; the sources of her poetic inspiration dried up. With the exception of three short poems, none of which was longer than twenty lines, she was to publish no poetry at all after this; if she wrote more, she cannot have considered it worth preserving, for there exists nothing dated after 1946, even in manuscript, except a short farewell poem to a housekeeper who left her service in 1948.

The years covered by this chapter—1930 to 1946—saw a great development in V S-W's prose. It was during these years that she wrote three of her best novels: *The Edwardians, All Passion Spent* and *The Dark Island.* Even more noticeable, however, was the advance made in biography. From the fairly simple studies of Aphra Behn and Andrew Marvell made in the late twenties she had progressed to the much more detailed *Saint Joan of Arc* and *The Eagle and the Dove,* which, quite apart from the fact that they had necessitated a considerable amount of research and thought, are written with a maturity and skill far above that displayed in her earlier biographies.

Although one of her best-known poems, *The Land,* had already been published by 1930, the period shows her continued poetic development. It is, like the biography, closely connected to her spiritual development. 1946 saw the end of her career as a poet; *The Garden* being the last flowering of her poetic talent.

V S-W herself appears to have passed through a period of somewhat troubled development during which she evinced a growing interest in religion and religious problems, which she clearly studied in some detail in the late thirties and early forties. Finally, however, she seems to have suffered some spiritual upheaval which resulted in the loss of some of the religious convictions she seems to have built up during the previous few years, leaving her full of doubts and uncertainties.

[119] The complete text of this unpublished poem will be found on p. 119 infra.
[120] Stevens, op. cit., p. 53.

The Years 1947 to 1962

V S-W published two books in 1947: *Nursery Rhymes,*[1] and *Devil at Westease.*[2] The first of these is a rather light piece of work dealing in a humorous manner with the origins and meaning of some well-known English nursery rhymes. The last four pages contain some reflections upon poetry and criticism.

Devil at Westease, which was published only in the United States, hinges upon an extreme case of duality, a true Jekyll and Hyde personality. Although duality is, as we have seen, a motif that occurs in several of her works of fiction, it is treated quite differently in this book. In earlier novels her attitude to duality appears to have been an unconscious one; an aspect of personality, possibly subconsciously introduced into the story, which she wished to grapple with and investigate for her own benefit. In *Devil at Westease,* however, the motif is treated quite objectively; the fact that Wyldbore Ryan and Professor Warren are really the same person is the key to the solution of the mystery, as Ryan and Warren provide each other with alibis which collapse when it becomes clear that they are not two separate persons.

This objectivity on V S-W's part would seem to indicate that she has come to terms with the conception of duality and that it worries her no more. There are, however, traces of ambivalence still left. As Ryan appears in the role of Warren for technical reasons only, that is to provide him with an alibi for the murder, he should be perfectly aware of the fact that Warren does not exist. In fact, the way in which Ryan refers to Warren, even when he has admitted that the man is a fiction, gives the reader the impression that in some way he really does feel that Warren has a life of his own. "I'm no criminal," he retorts when taxed with the deception, "that was the Professor".[3]

The book is not only a detective story but also demands, both of the author herself and of her readers, the answer to an ethical question: what are the relative values of the man of creative genius and the ordinary, non-productive citizen? Provided that no one else will suffer if he keeps silent, how should a man act who is the only person to know that a productive artist of the very highest ability has been guilty of murdering a man of the people? Should he speak out or not? In order to pose this question in the framework of the story she has chosen, V S-W has to reverse the normal Jekyll and Hyde situation, making Wyldbore Ryan, the amoral man, the basic character, and Warren, the kindly old professor, merely a role into which Ryan slips when the mood or occasion arises. Rather courageously V S-W thus makes the man for whose life she pleads an unsympathetic character, not a pleasant one. It is some measure of her skill

[1] Dropmore Press, London, 1947.
[2] Doubleday, New York, 1947.
[3] *Devil at Westease,* p. 192.

that a reviewer described the book as having a "subtle and original turn of plot", and concluded by saying "The solution is fantastic but perfectly fair to the reader; a satisfactory ending to a puzzler of exceptional charm and finish."[4]

1947 marked the beginning of a long period during which V S-W's creative ability seemed to desert her almost entirely. From the middle of 1947 up to the beginning of 1953, more than five years, she published nothing except a few magazine articles on various subjects. However, in January 1947, she did make a start on a work of some importance. It was the life of Anne Marie Louise d'Orleans, Duchesse de Montpensier, 1627—1693—La Grande Mademoiselle. In spite of the fact that "she isn't *quite* my sort of thing"[5] there were aspects of her story that V S-W found interesting:

> Her own description of herself is fascinating as a psychological document. It is a study in self-delusion by a most sincere person. It is on these lines that I shall try to base my portrait of her. You see, she persuaded herself that she had no worldly ambition, yet spent half her time trying to marry Kings or Emperors, and it was only when she fell in love with Lauzun that she came round to her own conception of herself as a person without ambition. A very interesting character.[6]

However, the book did not progress well, and it appears to have been laid aside soon afterwards, not to be resumed until 1953. It was not finished until 1959, twelve years after it was begun.

For H.N. the end of the war had meant several changes. He lost his seat in Parliament in the Labour landslide of 1945, and was given notice to leave his chambers in King's Bench Walk the same year; they were required for practising barristers. In 1946, he had moved his address in London to Neville Terrace, South Kensington, and in February 1947, he joined the Labour Party. He was invited to stand as Labour Candidate in North Croydon in the 1948 by-election. His defeat there was virtually the end of his political career, and after that he devoted most of his time to writing and literature. In 1948, he was invited to write the official biography of King George V. He accepted, and in 1952 completed the life, his magnum opus, for which he received a knighthood in 1953.

Ironically enough, although V S-W was never to write any more poetry and was temporarily unable to write prose, it was now that honours began to descend on her. True, the value of *The Land* had immediately been recognised and she had been awarded the Hawthornden Prize in 1927; now she was given the Heinemann Prize for *The Garden*. In December 1947, she was made a Companion of Honour for her services to literature.[7] In 1949, she was appointed to the bench as Justice of the Peace at Cranbrook, and the same year took her seat on the National Trust's Gardens Committee and on the Executive of the Society for the Preservation of Rural Kent. She was also invited by the British Council to make lecture tours for them; in February and March 1948, she was in Morocco, Algeria and Tunisia which, incidentally, provided a neat solution to the difficulty of her non-appearance on the platform during H.N.'s electoral campaign in North Croydon.[8] Then in 1949 she went to Spain, her "half-native land", for the British Council.[9] This was a source of great pleasure to her as she was able to

[4] *New York Times, Book Review*, 11 May, 1947, p. 31.
[5] *Diaries and Letters, 1945—62*, p. 88.
[6] *Ibid.*, p. 88.
[7] *Ibid.*, p. 117. See also *The Times*, 1 January, 1948, p. 6.
[8] *Ibid.*, p. 124.
[9] *Ibid.*, p. 161.

visit places she had written about in *The Eagle and the Dove* and *Pepita*. When, for example, she looked at the list of places she was to visit, she found that she was to lecture on modern English literature at Malaga, she exclaimed, "Now supposing Pepita, as a little *muchacha* in Malaga, could have had a glimpse into the future, and foreseen her granddaughter not as 'a bird in the air' but as a lecturer on a platform, wouldn't she have been incredulous and surprised? How Virginia [Woolf] would have appreciated this!"[10]

However, all this recognition was no compensation to her for the fact that she was unable to write:

> I am really rather depressed by my inability to write the simplest thing. No, let me be truthful, I am not 'rather depressed', but mortally depressed. I am like a motor-car that has been standing in a cold garage and refuses to give out even one little *pétard* of a firing-spark. I daresay it will warm up again some day, but meanwhile it is as cold as a frog.[11]

This was in January 1950. In December the same year, however, she was able to write in quite a different tone:

> Darling, I must write you another little note just to say how happy I am writing. It does make the whole difference in life. I just tell you this, because I like sharing things with you. I have been so miserable in the last two or three years, not being able to write; really worried I have been, thinking that it was gone from me for ever.[12]

The book that she was working on was *The Easter Party*.[13] But although she had begun to write again, progress was slow judged by her previous production, for it was not published until January 1953, more than two years later. This was a considerable time for V S-W to have spent on a novel of only one hundred and ninety pages when one considers that *All Passion Spent* and *The Dark Island*, both of about three hundred pages, were written in about ten months each. When the book finally appeared in January 1953, it was ridiculed in a sarcastic review by Marghanita Laski:

> After such triumphs of the novelist's art as *The Edwardians* and *All Passion Spent*, it must be confessed that Miss Sackville-West's *The Easter Party* is disappointing. The story of the eminent Q.C. who allows himself neither to feel human affections nor to consummate his marriage, but is at last brought to his senses through a threat to his beloved Alsatian dog seems to lack both the psychological probability and (surprisingly in view of Miss Sackville-West's previous achievements) a coherent integral shape. There are, however, some pleasing and evocative descriptions of gardens, and a fascinating side-track, unfortunately not fully explored, in the lovely Lady Quarles, who, when she experiences panic fear, smells goat.[14]

As this review appeared in *The Observer*, the newspaper to which both V S-W and H.N. contributed regularly, and as it was one of the first reviews to be published, it cut deep, more particularly as this was the first book she had been able to write for a long time. V S-W was not, however, the sort of person to give up on meeting the first reverse; she was made of sterner stuff:

> My poor Viti is hurt by a review of her new novel [*The Easter Party*] by Marghanita Laski, which is contemptuous and wounding. When such things occur to me,

---

[10] *Ibid.*, p. 164.
[11] *Ibid.*, pp. 183—4.
[12] *Ibid.*, p. 195.
[13] Michael Joseph, London.
[14] *Observer*, 25 January, 1953.

I become depressed and miserable. But Viti just gets angry, which I suppose is better.[15]

In actual fact, the story of the book is a very complex one which can by no means be dismissed as facilely as this reviewer did. Another critic showed much greater perspicacity when he pointed out that "something of all the preoccupations of Miss Sackville-West's earlier books has been brought into play, not omitting *The Eagle and the Dove*. ... *The Easter Party* is therefore interesting not only in isolation, but as a development of the outlook which produced *The Edwardians*." After commenting on V S-W's attitude to the English social structure, this critic goes on to add that what she is concerned with in the present book is the mental aura of Sir Walter Mortibois, Q.C.:

It hinges on the character of Sir Walter Mortibois, in whose name certain legal colleagues saw an apt pun: 'dead wood'. Mortibois, professionally in the thick of the human struggle, is privately wary of emotional entanglements. He is a man who could propose to the woman of his choice, saying, 'My heart is in no way engaged.' He sought a bargain with her for companionship but not love. Rose, a daughter of the parsonage, accepted, not for money or position, but because, paradoxically, she had fallen in love with him. On their honeymoon in the warm south he lectures her on the heavenly bodies, and that is all that is bodily in their relationship. At this point the reader may ask, is Mortibois human? It is a tribute to Miss Sackville-West's skill that he is credible, even exasperatingly so. His is a complex character, and every facet as presented is in itself credible. ... We have been presented with a picture of Walter in his room in the small hours of that morning when 'his secretive nature loved the privacy and solitude'. We find him reading, of all books, *The Cloud of Unknowing*, St. Augustine, St. John of the Cross. To these books, we are told, 'he returned over and over again.' ... We now deduce in him something earnestly enquiring, unsatisfied, perhaps self-tormenting, behind all his logical pessimism and cool detachment. ... He is still, the reader feels, a character groping after realization, after reality. This is not to say he does not live here: unreal people are not only those in books.[16]

Near the end of the review comes the observation, "Ultimately what her work poses is a religious question." This is perhaps the key to a full understanding of what V S-W is attempting to express. A careful study of the book brings to light certain facts which seem to indicate that the theme of the book is similar to that of *The Garden;* the conflict in a soul searching for God, and torn between Christianity on one side and paganism or pantheism on the other. Walter Mortibois is a man in whom "a sense of the suffering and folly of the human race flowed ceaselessly as a burning accompaniment to the blood in his veins. ... In another age and in another country he might have chosen the contemplative life."[17] When the demands of his profession make it necessary for him to take a wife, he seeks out a suitable girl very carefully and, when proposing to her, warns her that "I want my marriage to be a marriage in name alone. You understand what I mean?"[18] He wishes to give her no explanation of his reasons for dictating this condition, but adds:

I can at least assure you of two things; that they are in no way discreditable, and that they have no connection with my health. ... It is merely that I should not

[15] *Diaries and Letters, 1945—62*, p. 236.
[16] *Times Literary Supplement*, 6 February, 1953, p. 88.
[17] *The Easter Party*, pp. 49—50.
[18] *Ibid.*, p. 55.

prefer to disclose, at present, what is after all only a personal idiosyncrasy but one which is very deeply associated with my private philosophy of life.[19]

He never does tell his wife, but the reader, aware, as Rose is not, of Walter's deep interest in the mystics, and observing phrases used about him, such as "his chosen celibacy"[20] may come to the conclusion that his celibacy may have something in common with that of the religious recluse.

It is not, however, quite as simple as that. Juliet, the notorious Lady Quarles, introduces another element into the story. She, who describes herself as old and shop-soiled, is, despite her well-earned reputation, essentially a figure of innocence. "There was something nymph-like about Juliet, untarnished despite the life she had left and the many hands through which she had passed."[21] The reason is that she stands quite outside Christian morality; "her pantheism instinctive; without effort she identified herself with the pebbles of her brook, the leaf fallen on her path."[22] But she is also the focal point through which Panic powers can manifest themselves, and, as such, a symbol of sexuality. As it is clear that she holds a great fascination for Walter, the Pan motif seems to suggest that his celibacy is not only a voluntary abstinence similar to that of the Christian mystic, but is also connected with a fear of sexuality itself. The strange incident in the grotto,[23] and its sequel, when Walter discovers that the clock in his wife's room has stopped at the precise moment at which the manifestation in the grotto took place,[24] might be taken as being a demonstration to Walter of the strength of the powers with which he will have to contend if he chooses the Christian path.

During a conversation with Walter's brother, Gilbert, an eminent brain surgeon, Rose voices a thought that Juliet had already expressed forcibly to Walter when she said, "Walter darling, have you no heart to protect? Have you never suffered? Are you not afraid that some day you may be called upon to suffer?"[25] Rose also shows Gilbert the weak points in Walter's armour when she says that "there are only two things he cares for: Svend and Anstey"[26]—his dog[27] and his house.

Throughout the book, emphasis is given to the fact that it is Easter time; at various times almost all the principal characters comment pointedly on it,[28] which would seem to indicate that V S-W wishes to draw the reader's attention to the significance of some aspect of Easter. The most obvious aspect to choose would be redemption through an external agency.

On Easter Day, Gilbert, to whom Rose had said, "You are both practical men, you and Walter, but you, Gilbert, have something Christ-like about you",[29] persuades Walter to hand Svend over to him for an operation which, while being of the greatest value to mankind, will inevitably result in the death of the dog. Now Walter learns what suffering really is.

On Monday night, Rose discovers when she happens to look at the fireplace in the hall that, perhaps thrown off balance by the shock of losing Svend, "for once, Walter must have neglected to pile up the ashes."[30] During the night the house catches fire

---

[19] *Ibid.*, p. 55.
[20] *Ibid.*, p. 95.
[21] *Ibid.*, p. 70.
[22] *Ibid.*, pp. 97—8.
[23] *Ibid.*, pp. 88—9.
[24] *Ibid.*, p. 94.
[25] *Ibid.*, p. 81.
[26] *Ibid.*, p. 120.
[27] Svend is based on V S-W's Alsatian, Rollo (See supra, p. 25.)
[28] *Ibid.*, pp. 96, 100, 103, 113.
[29] *Ibid.*, p. 121.
[30] *Ibid.*, p. 160.

and is burnt to the ground. But, although Walter has at one blow lost the two things that were dearest in life to him, "he seemed transformed, a different man, a man suffering a violent form of catharsis, a purging, an experience."[31]

Viewed in this light, *The Easter Party* would seem to be an exposition of the religious and moral problems confronting V S-W, to which an arbitrary solution has been provided. This solution, which is basically Christian, appears to be different to the one that would have resulted from the premises in *The Garden*, which tended to be more pantheistic than Christian.

Soon after the publication of *The Easter Party*, V S-W resumed work on *Daughter of France*, which had been laid aside since 1947. "I revive the idea of writing about La Grande Mademoiselle", she wrote in her diary in March 1953.[32] She struggled on with the book through 1954 and 1955 although she felt that La Grande Mademoiselle had begun to dominate her life in an intolerable manner: "The Big Miss stands behind me with a whip", was the way she felt about it at times.[33] But progress remained very slow. It was not made quicker by the fact that she had been suffering from arthritis during these years, and now, in March 1955, damaged her back in a fall.[34] Then, in the autumn of 1955, an American, Francis Steegmuller, published his biography of La Grande Mademoiselle,[35] which received very favourable reviews. V S-W was greatly distressed, fearing that all her work had been in vain, and for a time contemplated giving up the book altogether.[36]

About a year after this, in January 1957, V S-W and H.N. went on the first of the winter cruises they were to make every year after this up till 1961. They had, for some years before this, been in the habit of going off together for a month's tour of some country, usually France or Italy, but sometimes Great Britain. The winter cruises began to be the time when V S-W did a large part of her writing. The first cruise was to Cape Town, Singapore and Java. During the two months they were on board, V S-W managed to write a considerable amount:

> V. has written some 40,000 words of *La Grande Mademoiselle,* but does not think she will be able to finish the book by the time we get back to England. And then will come all those interruptions and the Mademoiselle will be put away into a drawer until the long dark autumn evenings come. She does not, I fear, possess my gift of concentration, being so polite to those who intrude upon her that she becomes distracted ... her sublime patience with dawdlers ends by wearing her down.[37]

The following winter, 1957—1958, saw them on a cruise to the Caribbean, Panama and the Pacific coast of South America. Not so much was written on this trip, as V S-W was ill for part of the time.[38] However, on 13th August, 1958, she could say:

> Do you know what happened at 9.30 last night? La Grande Mademoiselle died, aged 63. This does not mean that I have not still got a lot to do, but the book is so to speak finished, and another month should clear it up. Ouf![39]

Nevertheless the book was not published until the end of March the following year. It might be called her magnum opus in prose; none of her other books had taken her

[31] *Ibid.,* p. 165.
[32] *Diaries and Letters, 1945—62,* p. 237.
[33] *Ibid.,* p. 255.
[34] *Ibid.,* p. 280.
[35] *La Grande Mademosielle,* Hamish Hamilton, London, 1955.
[36] *Diaries and Letters, 1945—1962,* p. 291.
[37] Harold Nicolson, *Journey to Java,* Constable, London, 1957, p. 218.
[38] *Diaries and Letters, 1945—62,* p. 341.
[39] *Ibid.,* p. 351.

anything like so long to write, and for none of her other books did she have to study such quantities of material. As the *Times Literary Supplement* points out:

> Her story is to be found in contemporary sources so copious as to appear positively horrifying. At first glance it would seem that Everybody who was Somebody at the courts of Louis XIII and XIV wrote memoirs, kept a diary or sent off a quantity of letters every week. Mademoiselle herself left a voluminous although patchy autobiography; yet this part of Miss Sackville-West's material is a drop in the ocean of personal records provided by courtiers, priests, valets, ladies-in-waiting, soldiers, physicians, and statesmen. Apparently unembarrassed by this stupendous richness, the author of *Daughter of France* has plunged into the flood, extricated her heroine adroitly and without fuss, administered artificial respiration, wrung out her pseudo-classic draperies, thrown away the disguising weeds, and set her up as it were on the right bank of history, for all to see.[40]

The reasons why V S-W chose to write this biography seem to have been quite different from those that led her to write the lives of Saint Joan and the two Teresas. In the case of the three saints her interest appears to have been fundamentally in their actions and in the reasons why they acted as they did, rather than in the personality of the women themselves, although the latter was naturally not ignored. In other words, it was the abstract religious aspects of their lives that she was mainly concerned with.

In *Daughter of France*, on the other hand, V S-W's interest seems to be far more in the personality, the character and the background of La Grande Mademoiselle. Although V S-W explicitly states that "*Le Grand Siècle* is not quite me somehow",[41] she moves in it with as much ease and understanding as if she felt herself to be a direct descendant of the courtiers of Louis XIV. There are some aspects of Mademoiselle's character that V S-W seizes upon with especial interest, for example her love for and trust in her worthless father, Gaston, who is presented as being an amusing and affectionate father to her, at least during the years of her childhood. There were, in fact, quite a number of points in which there was a decided resemblance between the writer and her subject. Both came from an aristocratic background and were keenly conscious of the fact; both suffered from not having been born boys; both had a real love of castles and shared an interest in building and architecture: there was a great deal about Mademoiselle with which V S-W could identify herself. However, although V S-W makes much of those sides of her character and circumstances that she finds appealing, this does not mean that she was blind to her weaknesses. Far from it:

> It is primarily as a splendiferous figure of fun that she is depicted by her new biographer. True, Miss Victoria Sackville-West is warmly attached to her endearing heroine; but the portrait she has drawn is that of an over-excitable maiden aunt —'clumsy', 'tactless' and 'shallow-pated', bound to make a fool of herself, whether she dabbled in warfare and political intrigue or fell a victim to romantic passion.[42]

Right from the beginning V S-W makes it quite clear that her clumsy, touching heroine is marked down for failure in life, in spite of all the advantages with which she was born. She does not attempt to excuse La Grande Mademoiselle, or to conceal the fact that she was in many respects a slightly ridiculous figure; "her clear-sighted criticisms, amounting sometimes to condemnation, are so cunningly infiltrated that the reader begins at last to take Mademoiselle's side against her [V S-W]".[43] Nevertheless,

[40] *Times Literary Supplement,* 8 May, 1959, p. 267.
[41] *Diaries and Letters, 1945—62,* p. 88.
[42] *Observer,* 5 April, 1959, p. 21.
[43] *Times Literary Supplement,* 8 May, 1959, p. 267.

the extent to which V S-W was in tune with Mademoiselle enabled her to present a picture of her that is both pathetic and endearing, and brings out to the full "the simple, touching grandeur of the unselfconscious and the sincere".[44]

Even before *Daughter of France,* appeared in print, V S-W had commenced work on her last novel, *No Signposts in the Sea.*[45] Most of the book was written, appropriately enough, on board ship, for it was begun in January 1959, on the Nicolsons' annual cruise,[46] that year to Tokyo and Saigon, and the bulk of the writing was done on the cruise in January and February 1960, to South Africa.[47] Twice work on the novel was interrupted by illness; V S-W suffered from severe attacks of virus pneumonia for two months in the summer of 1959, and again the following summer, with the result that the book was not finished until the autumn of that year, and was not published until early 1961.

The *Times Literary Supplement,* in its review, points out that the theme of the book is one that V S-W has dealt with before:

> Years ago, in *All Passion Spent,* Miss Sackville-West wrote about an old lady waiting serenely and peacefully for death. Her new novel, ... explores further the idea that acceptance of one's end obliterates self-pity and fear. It is in the form of a diary written during a Far-Eastern cruise by Edmund Carr, a middle-aged political columnist who knows he will never return to the hurly-burly of power-struck society. He has chosen to spend his last weeks in the company of the one woman he has ever loved, though determined she shall never know his feelings or his fate.[48]

The other motif arises out of his secret love for Laura. The book is a brilliant account of how Carr, who, near the beginning of the voyage can say to Laura with unconscious irony, "I have never known the meaning of jealousy",[49] gradually becomes its victim to the extent that, by jealousy and his own inferiority complex, he is totally blinded to the fact that she is in love with him. He interprets her hints at the truth as referring to the man he supposes to be his rival, the hated Colonel Dalrymple.

As might be expected, the book is more than a record of Edmund Carr's reflections on his approaching death combined with a beautifully written love-story. It appears also to be a summing up, addressed to H.N., of V S-W's married life, the principles that have guided it, and the success that it has been. For her, the essentials of a successful marriage appear to be a certain reticence and the necessity for both man and wife to share the same sense of values.[50] Speaking through Laura, V S-W adds:

> There is nothing more lovely in life than the union of two people whose love for one another has grown through the years from the small acorn of passion into a great rooted tree. Surviving all vicissitudes, and rich with its manifold branches, every leaf holding its own significance. ... Such a love can be achieved only by the practice of mutual respect and personal liberty.[51]

As an illustration of what she means, she quotes the following lines:

[44] *Ibid.,* p. 267.
[45] Michael Joseph, London, 1961.
[46] *Diaries and Letters, 1945—62,* p. 361.
[47] *Ibid.,* p. 377.
[48] *Times Literary Supplement,* 10 February, 1961, p. 85.
[49] *No Signposts in the Sea,* p. 35.
[50] *Ibid.,* p. 87.
[51] *Ibid.,* p. 89.

Let there be spaces in your togetherness
And let the winds of heaven dance between you.

Sing and dance together and be joyous and let each one of you be alone,
Even as the strings of a lute are alone though they quiver with the same music.

Stand together, yet not too near together;
For the pillars of the temple stand apart
And the oak tree and the cypress grow not in each other's shadow.[52]

This atmosphere of summing up together with the preoccupation with the nearness of death that permeate the whole story make it difficult not to believe that the book is a conscious leave-taking of this world in general, and H.N. in particular. There is no other evidence that V S-W was aware in 1960 of her approaching death. On the other hand, the fact that she tried to conceal from H.N. that she had a serious hæmorrhage in January 1962,[53] makes it doubtful whether she would have given any clearer indication of her knowledge than is contained in *No Signposts in the Sea*, even if she had been aware of how short a time remained.

In the book there is one passage in which there can be little doubt that V S-W is describing in symbolic terms the meaning of life as she sees it, and the fact that death is an absolute end. It is where she gives an account of the Man Overboard practice that is rehearsed on board the ship one day in the tropics. A lighted canister of petrol has been dropped into the ocean to simulate the man who is supposed to have fallen overboard:

> Apparently they had no intention of trying to reach him; no lifeboat was lowered; they contented themselves with watching the canister carried further and further away on some unseen current. It all seemed to me as unintelligible as many other things in life. One could hope only that it made sense to someone in authority. Meanwhile it was pitiable to see that small object struggling to survive, quaking and abandoned in an inexplicable waste; the flame dwindled once, and I thought it had been extinguished, but it revived in the diminished flicker of a last determination. Then it came to the edge of the lagoon, was buffeted by the ridge of our wake, tossed desperately for a moment, and was gone for ever.
>
> There are no tombstones in the sea.[54]

The book contains yet another motif that is of importance in considering V S-W and her work. Just as Laura is presented as a touchstone by which standards of behaviour in marriage are to be tested, so Mervyn Dalrymple appears as a criterion to be used when judging standards of general behaviour. Again and again Edmund Carr, even in the middle of his fits of jealousy, measures his thoughts and actions by what the colonel would consider to be the right thing, for he cannot but admire him. "I wish that I could dislike the man I hate."[55]

It is interesting to see what sort of person V S-W has chosen to play this role. The virtues that are explicitly accorded to Colonel Dalrymple by Carr, his rival, are many and varied. "He is genuine and unself-conscious through and through; and so modest that if he had the V.C., which perhaps he has, he would be at pains to conceal it."[56]

---

[52] *Ibid.*, p. 90. It has not proved possible to trace the source of this quotation.
[53] *Diaries and Letters, 1945—62*, p. 405.
[54] *No Signposts in the Sea*, p. 48.
[55] *Ibid.*, p. 146.
[56] *Ibid.*, p. 82.

Carr considers him "by no means stupid or ill-informed"[57] and likes "the out-of-the-way information which he imparts from time to time without insistence ... [he] has used his eyes and kept his ears open."[58] In several places it is made clear that although Dalrymple is intelligent and well-informed,[59] he never parades his knowledge or is too intelligent—he is not "clever" in the sense that an Englishman would regard as being uncomplimentary. There is "a touch of rough poetry about him"[60] and he "can't stand the sight of a beast in distress"[61] He is, in fact, "so unmistakably English. Well-bred English".[62] The ideal portrait that emerges is thus that of the "best type of English gentleman", and all that he stands for.[63]

A love of England and Englishness is a very salient feature of V S-W's character. Partly, no doubt, this is because by birth and upbringing she was very conscious of belonging to the class of Englishman which for centuries has provided the material from which the history of England was woven. By blood, however, she did not belong wholly to this class, and an awareness of this may have made the need to identify herself with England stronger than it is in most people. There can be little doubt that in her father V S-W saw personified and idealised much of what she valued most in England and the English, for characters that bear a resemblance to him figure in many of her books. The greatest monument to her love and devotion to England is *The Land*, although this love runs through many of her works. The clearest expression of her ideal of the English gentleman is Colonel Dalrymple in *No Signposts in the Sea*.

There remains little to relate after the publication of her last novel in 1961. All that year V S-W enjoyed apparent good health, and was able to write a long short-story, which was published in a magazine.[64] In January 1962, however, she had a hæmorrhage in the train on the way down to Southampton, where they were to embark for their cruise to the West Indies. She made no mention of this to H.N. Even in her diary she wrote no more than *"Disastrous* journey. I am very worried and confide in E. [Edith Lamont]."[65]

On their return from the cruise, V S-W consulted a doctor. He advised an exploratory operation, which was undertaken on 1st March and revealed abdominal cancer. Although V S-W did make a partial recovery from the operation and was able to come downstairs again and see her garden in May, she complained that she seemed unable to get her strength back, and at the end of May she suffered a sudden relapse.

She died at Sissinghurst on 2nd June, 1962, and was buried a few days later in the Sackville crypt at Withyham.

[57] *Ibid.*, p. 25.
[58] *Ibid.*, p. 32.
[59] *Ibid.*, pp. 25, 55 and 77.
[60] *Ibid.*, p. 32.
[61] *Ibid.*, p. 54.
[62] *Ibid.*, p. 78.
[63] See supra, p. 17.
[64] "Interlude in Two Lives", *Woman's Own*, 24 and 30 March, 1962.
[65] *Diaries and Letters, 1945—62*, p. 406.

A Survey of the Criticism of V S-W's Works

During her lifetime V S-W attracted a good deal of attention as a novelist, a biographer and a poet, in England, America and on the Continent. Her books seem to have been reviewed by most of the important newspapers and literary magazines on both sides of the Atlantic, and were frequently also reviewed by continental newspapers, even when the book had not been translated.

In addition to reviews, some of them long and authoritative, several critical studies on her writing were published during her lifetime. The earliest of these were two which appeared in August 1923, one in England and one in America.[1] They were followed six months later by another, published in England.[2] As this was before V S-W had written any of the books for which she is chiefly remembered today, it seems to indicate that she was already regarded as a writer of some promise.

After the award of the Hawthornden Prize to *The Land* in June 1927, came a number of newspaper articles and interviews with V S-W.[3] Few of them have much critical value, but they attest to a growing interest in her works among the public.

Immediately after the publication of *The Edwardians* in 1930, Hugh Walpole wrote a critical article about V S-W's writing in *Bookman*, New York,[4] and this was followed the next year by another, signed J.S. Will in *Canadian Forum*.[5] In December 1934 Mario Praz wrote about her prose in *La Stampa*.[6] The next important article to appear was that written in 1940 by Richard Church. Originally it was published in the *Fortnightly Review*,[7] but was reprinted later in *Eight for Immortality*[8] a year later. This deals only with V S-W's poetry, as does the critical article by Jacques Vallette which appeared in *Mercure de France* in 1949,[9] after the publication of *The Garden*. In between these comes a German essay by Hans Wagenseil which deals mainly with V S-W's prose works.[10]

The best of the critical work, that by Richard Church[11] and Jacques Vallette on her poetry, and by Mario Praz, Hans Wagenseil and possibly Walpole on her prose,

---

[1] A.L. Carvillon in *World's Work*, XLII (1923), 221—2, and J. Fletcher Smith in the Boston *Evening Transcript*, 18 August, 1923.
[2] W.H. Chesson in *Bookman*, London, (February 1924), 243—4.
[3] See infra, pp. 125—6.
[4] September 1930, pp. 21—6.
[5] 1931, pp. 462—3.
[6] 5 December, 1934, later reprinted in *Chronache Inglesi*, Milan, I (1950—2), 287—90.
[7] CXLVIII (1940), 601—8.
[8] Dent, London, 1941.
[9] 1—III—1949, pp. 423—31.
[10] *The Gate*, Bremen, II (1948), 3—6.
[11] Poet, critic, author of *The Growth of the English Novel*, Oxford University Press, 1968.

must be given serious consideration, as must critical remarks made by such well-known figures as Annette Kolb, who described V S-W as "die Bukolikerin klassischen Zuges",[12] as well as serious reviewers such as Raymond Mortimer, Augusto Guidi, Peter Quennell and Desmond MacCarthy. Their opinions are given later in the relevant contexts and need not be discussed here.

As regards V S-W and her public, there can be no doubt that she was and is read, and widely read. Several of her books have been reprinted many times: for example, during the last three years, 1969—1971, *The Land* (1926), *The Edwardians* (1930), *All Passion Spent* (1931), *Saint Joan of Arc* (1936), *Pepita* (1937), *Daughter of France* (1959) and *No Signposts in the Sea* (1961) have all been re-issued.[13] It has proved impossible to find out exactly the number of copies of her books that have been sold, for the records of the Hogarth Press were lost during the war, and V S-W's American publisher, Doubleday and Co. Inc., refuse to release any figures, but as far as *The Edwardians* is concerned, it is possible to state that the sales were 30,000 copies for the first six months in England[14] and 80,000 copies for the first year in America.[15] It has been reprinted seventeen times in England, the German translation sold three editions (S. Fischer-Verlag, Berlin, 1931) in addition to which there was a Tauchnitz edition (Leipzig, 1931). The book has also been translated into Italian (Mondadori, Milan, 1952), French (Grasset, Paris, 1933) and Swedish (Bonniers, Stockholm, 1931).

The Land is now in its twenty-second edition and has sold, in England alone, approximately 100,000 copies.[16]

Apart from a long critical essay written in 1968 by Nancy MacKnight at Columbia University, New York,[17] no critical studies on the work of V S-W appear to have been published since her death nine years ago, "but this is probably due to the usual lull in interest that follows the death of a writer."[18] Eight standard histories of literature and similar works published since 1962 have, however, seen fit to include articles on V S-W,[19] as have standard works of reference in many countries.

[12] Quoted in the foreword to V. Sackville-West, *Aus meinem Garten,* Heimeran-Verlag, München, 1966, and also by Eugen Skasa-Weiß in his review of *Weg ohne Weise, Süddeutsche Zeitung.* München, 21 Sept. 1963.
[13] Letters from V S-W's English publishers to the present author.
[14] See supra, p. 55.
[15] This figure is given in Doubleday, Doran's *Confidential Bulletin,* New York, 1 August, 1931.
[16] Letter dated 17 September, 1971 from William Heinemann Ltd. to the present author. The letter adds, "A sale of over 50,000 copies of any book of poetry puts it in the best-seller class."
[17] "V. Sackville-West", an unpublished thesis.
[18] Letter dated 18 June, 1971, from Richard Church to the present author.
[19] See infra, pp. 125—6.

V. Sackville-West's Fiction

Before attempting to evaluate V S-W's fiction it will be necessary to recapitulate some of the argument given in previous chapters in order to arrive at a conclusion about what sort of fiction she wrote and why she wrote it.

V S-W does not seem to have been one of those people with an instinctive ability to seize instantly upon the vital point of an argument, or to work out easily the solution to a knotty problem. Her son, Mr Nigel Nicolson, says after mentioning that she had no desire to share the world of men, "nor had she the gift of logical reasoning".[1] This is perhaps somewhat harsh. It might be more accurate to say that logical reasoning was a process that she had to learn to use, and that it was a considerable effort for her to do so.

When confronted with some personal problem that affected her deeply, it seems unlikely, from what we know of her character, that V S-W was able to discuss it and obtain relief in that manner. As we have seen, her difficulty in establishing contact with other people was so great[2] that she would hardly have been able to avail herself of this form of catharsis. Of all the people in the world, H.N. was probably the only one with whom she could discuss almost anything, but even with him there were obviously subjects that she could not bring herself, or did not wish, to mention. As she points out in *No Signposts in the Sea*, reticence is a virtue that she values highly in marriage.[3] Clearly she did not normally discuss with him the book that she was working on at the moment, for she says herself, referring to when she was writing *No Signposts in the Sea*, "I thought how odd it was, you and I writing away in our little cabins, not knowing what the other was writing about, and then discovering it in print months later."[4]

Instead of discussing her deepest problems, what V S-W seems to have done is to write about them in her novels. As she was aware, she was of a passionate disposition,[5] the sort of person who would probably find it difficult to come to a true understanding of herself. However, by transferring the problem to a fictional character in a fictional situation, she could perhaps create for herself the possibility of placing sufficient distance between herself and the problem to enable her to regard it dispassionately and reach some logical conclusion. This appears to be what she did during her first period

---

[1] *Diaries and Letters, 1930—39*, p. 18.
[2] See supra, p. 25 and the unpublished poem, infra, p. 117.
[3] *No Signposts in the Sea*, pp. 87, 133—4.
[4] *Diaries and Letters, 1945—62*, p. 386.
[5] *Diaries and Letters, 1939—45*, p. 266.

of fiction writing, from 1919 to 1924.[6] These were the years when her mother had just left her father and was beginning to grow more and more eccentric, and also the years when she and H.N. lived through a serious crisis in their married life.[7] The fiction she wrote then, *Heritage, The Dragon in Shallow Waters, The Heir, Grey Wethers* and *Challenge,* are largely based on problems of heredity and duality, and an atmosphere of violence and revolt is noticeable in several, particularly in *The Dragon in Shallow Waters.*

Whether the inclusion in these early works of her deep-set fears and was intentional or not there seems no way of telling, but it may well have been half-consciously done. Conscious or unconscious, there is beneath the surface of the majority of these works an undercurrent of unrest and self-searching which a discerning reader is likely to catch. In *Seducers in Ecuador,* the last novel of the first period, even the casual reader could hardly fail to be aware that this is a complex story which is certainly about more than a voyage in the Mediterranean and a murder trial.

V S-W wrote no fiction between 1924 and 1930. When she returned to it with *The Edwardians, All Passion Spent* and *Family History,* it is a somewhat different kind of novel that we meet. Here there is little trace of introspection or of hidden depths; these are fairly open, straightforward stories. It is worth noting also that the first two are the novels that many critics consider her best; they are beyond question the most successful financially. *The Edwardians* became an immediate best-seller, and both this and *All Passion Spent* have gone through reprint after reprint, the latest being in 1970 and 1971 respectively, forty years after they were first published. The fourth novel of the second period, *The Dark Island,* strikes a different note. In this sombre book, the last work of fiction V S-W was to write for eight years, she paints a scene which, like those in her early novels, may give the reader a sense of dark emotions that are only partially revealed in the story.[8]

With the exception of *Daughter of France* and two works which appear in part to have the character of exorcism,[9] the remainder of V S-W's literary output is concerned, directly or indirectly, to a greater or lesser extent, with religious questions — various aspects of divine revelation; the existence of God; life after death. As regards her remaining fiction, *Grand Canyon, The Easter Party* and *No Signposts in the Sea,* a change seems to come over her writing. The difference that gradually becomes apparent in her writing might be described as the emergence in the novel of a thesis, or inner story, which might be very different from the plot.

It seems quite probable that it is the parallel existence of thesis and plot that L.A.G. Strong, writing in the *Spectator,* is referring to when, in a review of *The Easter Party,* he points out that:

> Every novel written by a poet is in one sense an allegory. If it moves him as a poet —and he has no business with it otherwise—its characters and scenes will bear more than their literal meaning. Like a poem, it will contain more than the poet is consciously aware of as he writes it. Miss Sackville-West's work has always had this double validity. Even where she is best conscious of her intentions, the truth of her work rings on more than one level.[10]

---

[6] Two of the periods in which V S-W wrote fiction are clearly defined: 1919—24 and 1930—34. During the third, 1942—61, novels appeared at irregular intervals.

[7] See supra, p. 32.

[8] See supra, pp. 61—3.

[9] *Pepita,* written after the end of her mother's influence over her, and *Devil at Westease,* which seems to mark the end of her concern with duality. See supra, pp. 72—3.

[10] *Spectator,* 6 February, 1953, p. 158.

L.A.G. Strong evidently takes the view that V S-W was probably not aware of the fact that the novels she wrote were capable of being interpreted at different levels. He may be right, and it would certainly be difficult to refute his opinion categorically. There are nevertheless small indications which might be cited as tending to show that, as far as the thesis contained in some of her novels is concerned, V S-W might have been conscious of the fact that they do contain more than appears on the surface, that they can be interpreted in more ways than one, and that she might even have intended this to be so.

One of the main reasons for suspecting that a thesis has not crept into V S-W's books without her knowledge is that it sometimes appears to be so carefully concealed. Whereas an attentive reader can hardly come to the end of *Heritage* without realising that the author is keenly interested in questions raised by mixed heredity, the same reader might easily close *The Easter Party* without having seen that, underneath the surface, this is a book concerned with religious problems. This is because the clues to the inner story, the thesis, are scattered through the book concealed in unobtrusive little pieces of information, incidents, comments, fragments of dialogue and other indications which, if carefully collected and pieced together, give a different picture from the main story of what the book is about.[11] For example, Sir Walter Mortibois, Q.C., now emerges as an austere man dedicated with monklike celibacy to the quest for a religious ideal according to which he can live.

In *No Signposts in the Sea,* V S-W appears to use the same technique as in *The Easter Party*. The phrase which gives the book its name[12] precedes and seems to act as a pointer to the more significant phrase "there are no tombstones in the sea"[13] in a way that could hardly be mere coincidence. Furthermore, the 'man overboard practice'[14] and Edmund Carr's burial at sea[15] bear too great a likeness to each other in description and significance for it to be accidental. These and other incidents seem to point to other values lurking beneath the surface.

The inclusion of a thesis in V S-W's work appears to date from *Solitude* (1938). This poem, the whole tenor of which is clearly religious, does not yield up its personal meaning until certain lines and passages are picked out and pieced together.[16] In this poem, these seem to be included in an arbitrary order which is not always the order in which they should logically be arranged; it is, however, not difficult to pick them out or to rearrange them. Both the poem itself and the personal reflections are religious in nature, and they blend into a harmonious whole.

In *The Garden,* on the other hand, the thesis, once again religious,[17] is not only quite different from the motif of the poem itself, but is also far better hidden. It is quite possible to read and appreciate *The Garden* without paying any regard to the thesis. If both are considered together, however, they will be found to harmonize well despite their apparent dissimilarity.

In between these two poems comes the novel *Grand Canyon*. The failure of this strange book is quite possibly due to V S-W's inability in this, her first attempt in a prose work, to fuse together thesis and plot. It is clear that this must be a much more difficult thing to do in a novel, which must have a plot, than in a poem, which need

---

[11] See supra, pp. 75—7.
[12] *No Signposts in the Sea,* p. 28.
[13] *Ibid.,* p. 48.
[14] *Ibid.,* pp. 47—8.
[15] *Ibid.,* p. 156.
[16] See supra, pp. 66—7.
[17] See Stevens, op. cit., pp. 41—53.

not. Although she succeeded much better in *The Easter Party,* it was not until she wrote *No Signposts in the Sea* that a fusion of the two was successfully accomplished. This she achieved by reducing plot to a minimum, a mere framework for her ideas.

In view of the above, it seems that V S-W could hardly be described as a popular novelist in the sense that her works were written with an eye to the reaction of her public. Two of her novels, however, *The Edwardians* and *All Passion Spent,* can be described as popular in the sense that they caught and retained general attention. In the majority of her books she seems rather to have written to satisfy personal needs, at least to a considerable extent.

It may seem strange that an author whose work is frequently of so personal an origin can allow her books to be published. A statement V S-W once made during an interview goes far towards explaining this. She could never, she said, discuss her work with others when she was writing it.[18] "I can't even mention it, or it gets tarnished. It's an intensely private matter. The minute it's gone to the publisher it's gone from you, and means nothing more to you."[19] Other authors have said much the same thing.[20]

The reviews of V S-W's fiction tend by and large to fall into one of three catagories: the positive, those which take her to task on some point, and the negative. Those which might be called 'painfully polite' are so few that they can be left out of consideration. The great majority of reviews are either positive, or positive in essence while criticising some aspect of the book. As far as the negative reviews are concerned, it is interesting to note that approximately fifty percent deal with *The Easter Party* or *No Signposts in the Sea.* In view of what has been said above, it seems that the reception accorded to these last works of fiction must have depended to a large extent upon whether the critic had realised what V S-W was trying to do in these books. The reviewer most positive to *The Easter Party,* for example, was also the one who had best understood her purpose.[21] One of the most negative made no attempt to do so, but used his review as a peg on which to hang ideas about which she had not written at all.[22]

The points dealt with by contemporary criticism may be summarized under several headings, the most important of which are: style and language, originality, individuality and force, the creation of character, atmosphere.

Language attracts comment in a large number of reviews in America, Great Britain and on the Continent. The majority bestow praise. "The sheer sustained beauty of her writing" is L.A.G. Strong's description,[23] while the *New York Times* speaks more soberly of "the fine prose employed by the author. . . . there are times when it moves with an almost lyrical note."[24] "Quel plaisir," states *Mercure de France* many years later, ". . . de lire une prose ferme, naturelle, digne, digne de la grande réputation de Miss Sackville-West."[25] Even in adverse criticism may be found remarks such as Andræ's comment about V S-W's "så påfallande stilistisk färdighet och så klar berättarbegåvning".[26] Adverse, however, was Raymond Mortimer's criticism of one of

---

[18] During the early 'twenties she did, however, show some of her poetry to Edward Marsh before publishing it, as her correspondence with him shows. See Christopher Hassall, *Edward Marsh: A Biography,* London, 1959, pp. 513—4.

[19] *Everyman,* 23 October, 1930, p. 392.

[20] For example, Somerset Maugham in the "Author's Preface" to *Cakes and Ale.*

[21] *Times Literary Supplement,* 6 February, 1953, p. 88.

[22] Staffan Andræ in *Dagstidningen Arbetaren,* 11 December, 1954, p. 4.

[23] *Fortnightly Review,* CXXXVI (1931), 132.

[24] *New York Times,* 18 February, 1923, p. 11.

[25] *Mercure de France,* July 1959, p. 527.

[26] *Dagstidningen Arbetaren,* 11 December, 1954, p. 4. ("such obvious stilistic skill and so clear a gift for narration.")

V S-W's early novels for "a certain sort of empty rhetoric". But, he added, "because [those to whom it is not agreeable] find Miss Sackville-West apparently revelling in banal eloquence, they will take it for granted that her mind is ordinary. And that will be a most regrettable mistake."[27] Twenty years later, however, his opinion of her writing had changed, and we find him referring to "her new and extremely well-written book."[28]

More definite than the frequently found "distinguished style" are comments such as the one made by Amy Lowell that V S-W "has a style which obeys her perfectly, and she understands how to keep her parts subordinate to her whole."[29] The simplicity and purity of her prose writing are stressed by several critics[30] and various other aspects of her style are pointed out by other reviewers. An Italian reviewer says, for example:

E' in effetti l'essenza e quintessenza di una tecnica tradizionale accettata e perfezionata ma senza introduzione di metodi nuovi, il meglio della 'conservazione', prodotto da un'aristocratica scrittrice di cui può dirsi che in lei l'educazione letteraria faccia tutt'una cosa col culto della tradizione: educazione e tradizione inglesi al cento per cento. Intanto, in questo come in altri libri della S.W. l'ambientazione risente non solo d'una consumata esperienza e consuetudine della villa e della campagna inglesi, includendovi l'edilizia rurale e l'architettura dei manieri, ma di una ricreazione e integrazione di tali aspetti, in cui trova posto anche il paesaggio della narrativa e della pittura inglesi; poi, una estensione di tale studio dell'ambiente a tipi umani spiccatamente inglesi e come tali assunti e riconoscibili. Nè il fatto contingente per quanto impressionante dell'ultima guerra ha potuto incidere in tale stile e costume narrativo.[31]

On the negative side must be counted a comment made in the *Times Literary Supplement*[32] that V S-W sometimes interrupts the flow of her prose with some irrelevancy which disturbs the attention of the reader. This is a valid remark; such interruptions do occur in several of her books.

Originality, individuality, forcefulness and boldness are qualities to be found in V S-W's writing, as a number of critics recognize. It is, amongst others, these qualities that Amy Lowell singles out for praise in her long review of *The Dragon in Shallow Waters*.[33] Other critics have seized on one or several of them, *Mercure de France*, for example, referring to her as "une femme, qui est aussi un grand poète et un écrivain original",[34] and the *New Statesman and Nation* commenting that "the independence one hoped for from the theme is precisely to be found in these pages."[35]

Related to these qualities is the question of resemblance between V S-W's writing and that of other authors. No less than six critics have pointed out that in her first novel, *Heritage*, she employed Conrad's literary device of telling a story by one person who uses, to a great extent, the monologue of another. One of them, writing in the *Observer*, adds that by doing so, "her own quality of directness absolute was fettered and entangled," but that in her second novel, "in throwing all that aside she finds herself and

[27] *New Statesman*, XXXIX (21 July, 1923), 448.
[28] *New Statesman and Nation*, XXVI (13 November, 1943), 319.
[29] *New York Times*, 26 March, 1922.
[30] *Times Literary Supplement*, 22 May, 1919; *Manchester Guardian*, 2 June, 1931; *Mercure de France*, 1—IX—1936, p. 424, and others.
[31] Augusto Guidi in *L'Italia che scrive* XXXVIII (1955), 33.
[32] 8 May, 1959, p. 267. See also the *Scotsman*, 11 June, 1936 (Review of *Saint Joan of Arc*), which presents a similar view.
[33] *New York Times*, 26 March, 1922.
[34] 1—IX—1936, p. 424.
[35] I (6 June, 1931), 547.

comes wholly to her own."[36] Of her later novels, *Grey Wethers* owes an unmistakable debt to *Wuthering Heights,* and *Seducers in Ecuador* reminds one of the short stories of Henry James. Except in these books, her originality and individuality led her to steer her own course to a large extent, independent of other writers.

Where characterization is concerned, opinions differ. On one hand she receives high praise from many writers: in Germany for "ein in der Feinheit und Innigkeit seiner Psychologie, der Vornehmheit und Grazie seines bewundernswerten Stils ungemein reizvollen Bildnisses vergangenen Adelsgenerationen";[37] in France, because "elle possède l'art de décrire avec attrait et de caractériser en peu de mots. La psychologie des personages est d'une pénétration surprenante et leurs actions et leurs gestes sont d'accord avec leur tempérament et leur mentalité";[38] in America, where three different reviewers in the *New York Times* have spoken in the highest terms of her character drawing;[39] in England, where critics in the *Times Literary Supplement* have on several occasions warmly praised her, once for her ability to "characterize in the real novelists' way—by allowing her characters to reveal themselves in speech and action",[40] and on others for fine portrayal of individual characters.[41]

On the other hand, her characterization is adversely criticised by some reviewers. Marghanita Laski's remarks on *The Easter Party,* in which she describes the story as seeming "to lack both the psychological probability and ... coherent shape" has already been quoted.[42] A Swiss critic commented that "Einleuchtende populär-psychologische Bemerkungen, die von nichts weiter als einer guten Beobachtungsgabe zeugen, machen keine Diktion weit ... Der als 'genial' und 'brilliant' apostrophierte Journalist Edmund Carr schildert seine Reiseerlebnisse in einer so tantenhaften Manier, dass man an der Brillianz, mit der er angeblich sein Metier beherrscht, zu zweifeln beginnt."[43] Other negative opinions are to be found.

One possible explanation for this divergence of opinion is indicated in a review of *The Easter Party.* "Miss Sackville-West's novel", says the critic, "is not a realistic story. ... Like the first English novelists, she has used realistic detail to document a fable".[44] V S-W's ability to characterize if she intends to do so is well documented by many reviewers, but is seems probable that in some of her fiction she is more concerned with other values. It is worth noting that she has given some of her characters names such as Clare, Bellamy, Temple, Mortibois, Shirin[45], which invite the reader to suspect the presence of allegory. If this is so, and some characters are intended to have an allegorical content, this need not in itself preclude them from bearing a remarkable resemblance to real human beings, but the necessity for them to do so decreases in inverse proportion to their allegorical significance. A failure to realize the purpose of one of her books might account for some negative criticism of her characterization.

Atmosphere and power of description are qualities in V S-W's writing that a number of critics have attested to. After stating that "the novel of atmosphere is among the

[36] *Nation* (London), 14 June, 1919; *Bookman* (London), June 1919; *Brooklyn Eagle,* 25 October, 1919; *Observer,* 5 June, 1921; *Evening Transcript,* (Boston), 27 August, 1919, and an article on V S-W by J. Fletcher Smith in the Boston *Evening Transcript,* 18 August, 1923.
[37] *Der Gral,* München, 26 J (1931—2), 293.
[38] *Mercure de France,* 15—VI—1920, p. 818.
[39] Amy Lowell, 26 March, 1922; Elizabeth Liman Brown, 12 June, 1932; Jane Spence Southron, 25 November, 1934.
[40] 16 June, 1921, p. 386.
[41] 28 May, 1931, p. 424; 11 October, 1934, p. 692; 30 October, 1937, p. 796; 6 February, 1953, p. 88.
[42] Supra, p. 74.
[43] *Die Weltwoche,* Zürich, 1 April, 1966.
[44] L.A.G. Strong in the *Spectator,* CXC (6 February, 1953), 158.
[45] Which is the Persian word for "sweet".

most difficult of all forms of fiction", one reviewer adds, "Miss V. Sackville-West, however, has learnt the true secret, and *Grey Wethers* is as sound and penetrating an example of its kind as any we are likely to encounter for many seasons to come".[46] Another goes so far as to say that "in her deep, imaginative sense of place and atmosphere resides Miss West's chief strength",[47] and several others make explicit reference to this aspect of her writing.[48] As regards her power of description, the *Times Literary Supplement* writes: "Finally, one must testify to the author's sense of style and power of description. It is not a mere knack of fine writing; its virtue lies in its essential sobriety, relying not so much on verbal opulence and high-flown imagery as in the power to select, and, in selecting to bestow thereby distinction and significance on the object selected. It is rare to possess such a power; not to be possessed by it is rarer still."[49]

The picture which emerges of V S-W as a novelist is of a writer possessing originality and individuality which prevent her from following well-trodden paths. She has a sense of style which rarely betrays her, power of description, an ability to create atmosphere and, when she wishes, to characterize well. Not a popular novelist in the sense that she wrote down to her readers—some of her works seem, on the contrary, to have been written more for herself than for the public—some of what she has written is nevertheless not only still worth reading but is, in fact, still read, as re-prints of her books show. Although "head and shoulders above the vast majority of her contemporaries",[50] she fails to reach the first rank of fiction writers because the universality which characterizes the work of the great novelists is not felt to be present in her writing. Sufficient time has not yet elapsed for her to be assigned a place amongst her contemporaries with any accuracy, but it seems that some of her novels at least will have to be taken into consideration by the future historian of literature when dealing with the fiction of the first half of the twentieth century.

[46] Arthur Waugh in the *Daily Telegraph*, 10 June, 1923.
[47] From a review of *The Heir* (1922) in the *Daily News*, London. The exact date of the review is unknown, but a photostat copy of the review is in the possession of the present author.
[48] Reviews of *Heritage* in *Bookman*, London, June 1919; *Bookman*, New York, 1919; review of *Grey Wethers* in the *Times Literary Supplement*, 23 June, 1923, p. 438; reviews of *Noble Godavary* in *Bookman*, London, July 1932; the *Observer*, 10 July, 1932.
[49] 16 June, 1921, p. 386.
[50] *New York Times*, 12 June, 1932.

V. Sackville-West's Biographical Works

"Biography", said Harold Nicolson in a lecture he gave in 1927, "was scarcely thought of, it had not even a name, before 1683; its legitimacy was hardly recognised before 1791; it possesses a most unfortunate heredity; it suffers from many congenital defects; and its collaterals behave with such frequent vulgarity as to bring it into disrepute. And yet English biography, in spite of its shabby relations and its mixed ancestry, is in fact a perfectly respectable branch of literature."[1] It is important to note that H.N. describes it as a branch of literature; indeed, it is so described in the *Oxford Dictionary*.[2] Dunn, writing only eleven years earlier, makes it clear that this is a comparatively modern view of biography, for he states that "it is only in recent times that histories of literature have recognised the claims of biography to equal rank with other forms of prose. We have accepted the poetry and the prose of English authors. ... We have scarcely deigned to acknowledge that... biographies may also be literature of a high order."[3]

Before attempting to set up standards by which one may evaluate English biography, other considerations than the literary merits of the work must of course be considered. Perhaps the most important of these is the division of biography into "impure" and "pure"; a distinction observed both by H.N. and by Dunn. The causes of "impure" biography are defined as "the desire to celebrate the dead, ... the desire to compose the life of an individual as an illustration of some extraneous theory or conception, ... undue subjectivity in the writer."[4] The essentials of "pure" biography are, firstly, "that of historical truth, by which is meant not merely the avoidance of misstatements, but the wider veracity of complete and accurate portraiture."[5] Secondly, "that it shall be well-constructed. ... I do not deny that an ill-written biography, if strictly true and furnished with sufficient detail, can both interest and delight. ... The 'pure' biography should stimulate a far deeper response."[6] Finally, "there must... be a consciousness of creation, a conviction that some creative mind has selected and composed these facts in such a manner as to give them a convincing interpretation; that, in a word, the given biography is a work of intelligence."[7]

The fact that biography must be judged on its own merits as an independent branch of literature was stressed even more heavily by Sir Sidney Lee, the editor under whose

---

[1] *The Development of English Biography*, London, 1927, p. 16 (Hogarth Lecture).
[2] "The history of the lives of individual men, as a branch of literature."
[3] Waldo Dunn, *English Biography*, London, 1916, p. 265.
[4] H.N., *op. cit.*, pp. 9—10.
[5] *Ibid.*, pp. 10—11.
[6] *Ibid.*, pp. 12—13.
[7] *Ibid.*, p. 13.

guidance the *Dictionary of National Biography* was completed, when he laid down in a Leslie Stephen Lecture that "any assistance that biography renders these three great interests—ethical, historical, and scientific—should be accidental; such aid is neither essential nor obligatory."[8]

Richard Altick, in a recent work on literary biography,[9] confirms these aims, at the same time going into a great deal of detail as to how they may be achieved. He defines some of the qualities which distinguish first-rate biography as the "ceaseless quest for the essence of the subject's character, the application of the biographer's experience of the world to the moral and psychological problems his narrative raises, the spirit of skepticism governed by common sense."[10] He also makes some remarks on the extent to which it is permissible for the biographer to appear in the work he is writing, concluding that he "should not draw attention to his presence by use of the first-person singular".[11]

If we accept the dicta expressed or implied in these works, we then arrive at a set of criteria by which we may judge the value of English biography. To summarize briefly, they are:

(a) It should not be written to illustrate some preconceived idea or theory, or to celebrate the dead.
(b) It should not be unduly subjective.
(c) It should be historically true to the spirit of the subject, not merely to the facts.
(d) It should be well-written, and should avoid giving prominence to the personality of the biographer.
(e) It should give a convincing interpretation of the subject.

One of the most fruitful sources of the kind of ethically didactic biography proscribed by the first criterion has, for reasons which must be obvious, always been hagiography. As two of V S-W's biographical works, *Saint Joan of Arc* and *The Eagle and the Dove,* deal with the lives of saints, it is here first and foremost that the presence of didactic tendencies might be suspected. A study of the books reveals, however, that the attitude with which she approaches her subjects is inquiring, not didactic. She does not assume that Joan's "voices" came from God, or that the miracles ascribed to Saint Teresa and Saint Thérèse are true; neither does she disbelieve, but examines the facts in an endeavour to reach a just conclusion. It is this openness of mind that Otto Karsten finds in *Saint Joan:*

> Frau Sackville-West entfaltet eindrucksvoll die spezifischen Tugenden angelsächsischer Geschichtsbetrachtung, nämlich eine von wohltuendem Freimut durchlüftete Vorurteilslosigkeit der Anschauung im Bunde mit einer gleichsam lateinischen Nüchternheit der Aussage.[12]

---

[8] *The Principles of Biography,* University Press, Cambridge, 1911, p. 18.
[9] *Lives and Letters: A History of Literary Biography in England and America,* New York, 1965. This interesting, if somewhat diffuse work, makes no systematic attempt to formulate criteria by which biography may be judged. Throughout the book, however, is to be found a great deal of useful guidance on what modern scientific criticism may profitably take into account. The main stress of the book is on the biographies of literary figures, which makes some of it inapplicable to other biographical works.
[10] *Ibid.,* p. 57.
[11] *Ibid.,* p. 376. Another work on biography which is useful when considering the portrayal of character, the conflicting aims of science and art, and the need for selectivity is John Garraty's *The Nature of Biography,* London, 1958.
[12] *Literatur,* Stuttgart, 39 J. (1936/7), 573.

A number of English reviewers also commented on this aspect of the work.[13]

The Eagle and the Dove is characterized by the same approach. Raymond Mortimer's remarks may be taken as representing much of the informed critical opinion on this point. "Two obvious ways to such a subject are open to the biographer," he wrote, "that of the Catholic and that of the rationalist. Miss Sackville-West has chosen the more difficult approach. Unguided by any preconception, except apparently some form of theism, she has examined her material with the utmost openness of mind."[14] One might have expected Catholic circles to react negatively to a non-Catholic writer expressing views on dogma, but the contrary proved to be the case. The critic writing in the *Catholic Herald* warmly recommended the book to his readers.[15]

What is true of V S-W's works on saints is no less true of her other biographical writing. None of it could be described as being written in order to illustrate some preconceived idea.

The second point included in the first criterion, the desire to celebrate the dead, is one that appears to be foreign to V S-W's temperament. None of her works is in any sense a commemorative volume; even in *Pepita,* V S-W never allows her admiration of her mother, for example, to blind her to the less attractive aspects of her character.

Undue subjectivity in the writer is a more difficult matter to assess. As H.N. points out, "to a certain extent a subjective attitude is desirable and inevitable; and indeed the most perfect of English biographies, such as Lockhart's *Life of Scott,* inevitably contain or convey a sketch of the biographer subsidiary to that of the central portrait."[16] Undue subjectivity might be said to exist where the biographer attributes to his subject ideas and attitudes which are, in reality, not the subject's own, but are reflections of the biographer's thoughts and personality.

All V S-W's biographical work is subjective in some degree; least in *Saint Joan of Arc* and *The Eagle and the Dove;* most, perhaps, in *Aphra Behn,* her first essay in the genre. It would, however, be difficult to contend that her subjectivity is undue. It is true that she sometimes deduces traits in her subject for which she can scarcely possess documentation, but she says quite openly that she is doing so, and the deductions she makes are entirely in character with the facts known about the subject. V S-W says herself that "it is enough if [the biographer] can persuade his reader to take his store of specific knowledge for granted, and allow him to proceed to a broader picture, the picture of Mrs Behn in her loose robe de chambre, a little slovenly perhaps, and often a little too coarse, but always generous and warm and kindly, writing away at her slap-dash dialogue in her sordid London room, interrupted by young Grub Street knocking at her door in the confidence that they will be met with jokes and sympathy and common-sense, and, if need be, with the help of a not too well-furnished purse."[17] This may be H.N.'s "wider veracity of complete and accurate portraiture" carried to extremes, but it is hardly undue subjectivity as defined above.

In her later biographical works, V S-W learnt to deduce with greater circumspection, but her deductions have always been in keeping with the character of the subject, even in her earlier works.

When considering the criterion of historical truth, greater clarity will be obtained if we observe H.N.'s distinction between factual accuracy and truth to the spirit of the

[13] For example, *Times Literary Supplement,* 6 June, 1936, p. 469; *Observer,* 7 June, 1936, p. 9; *Church Times,* 1 June, 1936; *Spectator,* CLVI (19 June, 1936), 1140.
[14] *New Statesman and Nation,* XXVI (13 November, 1943), 319.
[15] *Catholic Herald,* 12 November, 1943, p. 3.
[16] *The Development of English Biography,* p. 10.
[17] *Aphra Behn,* p. 12.

subject. As regards the former, very little is to be found in contemporary criticism, even in that written by informed reviewers. This may safely be construed as being positive criticism, since any inaccuracies here would quickly have been seized upon and exposed. The only comment which appears to single out factual accuracy is to be found in *Mercure de France* which, reviewing *Daughter of France,* remarks that the book gives "une occasion d'explorer les coulisses de notre histoire, souvent mal connues de nous, en suivant un guide avec lequel, si nos historiens ne tombaient pas toujours d'accord, ce ne serait que sur des points de détail."[18]

The facts about the subjects in three of V S-W's major biographies—Saint Joan, Saint Teresa, Saint Thérèse and La Grande Mademoiselle—are far too well-known to permit of much discussion. This, however, is not quite the case where her other works are concerned: one major biography about Pepita and her daughter, and two biographical sketches: *Aphra Behn* and *Andrew Marvell.* As regards *Pepita,* an appreciation of its factual accuracy will be found in Appendix A of this dissertation. *Aphra Behn* and *Andrew Marvell* are much slighter studies which did not attract a great deal of attention when they were published. No one, however, appears to have suggested that they contain any factual discrepancies.

If we turn from the historical accuracy of the subject itself to the accuracy of the background material, we find, at least as far as *Saint Joan of Arc* is concerned, one reviewer stating that "from distrust of herself or dislike of the bogy 'the historian', or probably through a mingling of both, she has taken little trouble about the history of the fifteenth century."[19] To this must be added the more specific, but related, complaint from the military correspondent of the *Evening Standard* that "I do not believe that the Maid, in her 14 months of high command, made any mistakes or gave proof of anything but the greatest qualities of leadership. When Miss Sackville-West finds fault with her—as she does on two occasions—she is demonstrably in error, largely because I think she has not familiarised herself sufficiently with military methods of the time."[20]

The *Evening Standard* military correspondent appears to be only partly right here; the book in no way denies her high qualities as a leader and secondly, as the *Times Literary Supplement* points out, "Miss Sackville-West contends, and we think proves, that at least in the early stages Joan was regarded by Dunois and the rest as a talisman rather than as a commander. She was not admitted to councils of war; she was actually informed only of such parts of the plans as immediately concerned her."[21] Nevertheless, there may be some justification in the criticism that V S-W had not paid sufficient attention to the historical background.

If there is little about factual accuracy in criticism of V S-W's works, there is much more about faithfulness to the spirit of the subject. "Elle reconstruit," writes *Mercure de France,* "avec une pénétrante subtilité le caractère de la paysanne de Domrémy et réussit à présenter au lecteur une Jeanne d'Arc telle qu'elle fut réellement."[22] Pamela Hansford Johnson commented that "she breathes far more life into her Joan by the simple statement of fact and by admissible reconstruction than was ever breathed by any of the Maid's more gaudy romancers;"[23] the *Church Times* adds that "the external life of Joan is known in great detail. It is followed here step by step, and during her

[18] Juillet 1959, p. 527.
[19] *Manchester Guardian,* 10 July, 1936, p. 7.
[20] Exact date unknown. (See p. 90, note 47 supra.)
[21] 6 June, 1936, p. 469.
[22] 1—IX—1936, p. 424.
[23] *Liverpool Daily Post,* 10 June, 1936.

months of public activity almost day by day. The book brings out with great force Joan's commonplace sanity and peasant shrewdness;"[24] and a Swedish reviewer, writing more than a year later, was able to sum up: "Med skäl har miss V. Sackville-Wests biografi över Jeanne d'Arc blivit erkänd och berömd som en av de utmärktaste, kanske den bästa biografien över den märkliga franska bondflickan från Domremy, ... hennes senaste biograf [hör] till de samvetsgranna, lärda, av sitt stora ämne gripna, men likväl fullt opartiska levnadsskildrarna."[25]

The Eagle and the Dove drew similar comments from reviewers. Sigrid Undset, for example, wrote that "Miss Sackville-West has portrayed Teresa's strong and sane and complex personality, on the face of it so full of contradictions, with understanding and unsentimental love."[26] On the other hand, another reviewer, while admitting that "Miss Sackville-West has read and absorbed so much of St. Teresa that she has not only woven into her book a great many of her most characteristic sayings but has assimilated much of her spirit," also criticizes the book because "it fails to penetrate. The real Teresa is to be found, neither in her *Letters,* nor in her levitations, but in the books of which Miss Sackville-West says least: her masterpiece, the *Interior Castle,* and two exquisite but little-known opuscules, the *Conceptions* and the *Exclamations.*"[27] Against this view must be set, as Sigrid Undset observes, the fact that "it would be impossible within the limits of such a book to give an impression of the full stature of the Spanish Teresa, ... Her writings are just touched upon—to go into them at any length would be outside the scope of the book."[28]

If, finally, we consider *Daughter of France,* we shall find much the same attitude among reviewers. Directly or indirectly, the majority express approval of the portrait of La Grande Mademoiselle it contains. "Apparently unembarrassed by this stupendous richness [of material]," writes the *Times Literary Supplement,* "the author of *Daughter of France* has plunged into the flood, extricated her heroine adroitly and without fuss, administered artificial respiration, wrung out her pseudo-classic draperies, thrown away the disguising weeds, and set her up as it were on the right bank of history, for all to see. Mademoiselle walks—strides, rather—in a clear, even light: we hear her voice: we share in her triumphs and her defeats."[29]

If we turn to the literary merits of V S-W's biographical works, there can be little doubt what the verdict must be. Review after review contains such expressions as "the lovely, sensitive and unaffected writing";[30] "écrit en un style limpide et simple qui en rend la lecture fort agréable";[31] "The book has a charm and grace and wisdom as impossible to classify as its subject";[32] "her new and extremely well-written book";[33] "Lovers of good books will find *The Eagle and the Dove* exquisitely integrated and beautifully fabricated";[34] "quel plaisir, sur un sujet pareil, d'échapper aux clichés du

[24] 1 June, 1936.
[25] Ivan Oljelund in *Svenska Dagbladet,* 16 October, 1937. ("Miss Sackville-West's biography of Jeanne d'Arc has justly been recognized and praised as one of the most excellent, perhaps the best, biography of the remarkable French peasant girl from Domremy ... her latest biographer is among those conscientious, learned writers of lives who are moved by their great subject, but are nevertheless completely impartial.")
[26] *New York Times,* 20 February, 1944, p. 3.
[27] E. Allison Peers in the *Guardian,* 31 December, 1943.
[28] *Loc. cit.*
[29] 8 May, 1959, p. 267.
[30] Review of *Saint Joan of Arc* by Pamela Hansford Johnson in *Liverpool Daily News,* 10 June, 1936.
[31] Review of *Saint Joan of Arc* in *Mercure de France,* 1—IX—1936, p. 424.
[32] Review of *Pepita* in *Spectator,* 19 November, 1937, p. 24. (L.A.G. Strong).
[33] Review of *The Eagle and the Dove* by Raymond Mortimer in *New Statesman and Nation,* XXVI (13 November, 1943), 319.
[34] New York *Herald Tribune,* 27 February, 1944.

genre et de lire une prose ferme, naturelle, digne, digne de la grande réputation de Miss Sackville-West."[35]

The one blemish which is liable to be found now and again in V S-W's prose writing —the irrelevant and disturbing comment previously mentioned in this dissertation[36]— appears in *Saint Joan of Arc*[37] and also in *Daughter of France*.[38] This criticism does not, of course, apply to the perfectly legitimate and helpful intrusion of the author into the narrative to explain some point, or even to give his own views upon some matter. It refers rather to unjustified or uncalled-for comment.

Remarking on the second instance mentioned above, the *Times Literary Supplement* wrote that "when we have been transported—and so agreeably—into Mademoiselle's world, it is unpleasant to be removed from it in this abrupt way. Such flaws are minor and infrequent; they do not spoil the book: but now and then they hold up the flow of the narrative. ... In a less well composed biography such lapses of tact would not be worth mentioning. Miss Sackville-West's standards are so high that the smallest fault is apt to stay in the memory."[39] In the instances cited above, it seems that the personality of the author has intruded too much into the narrative of the biography.

It is, as might be expected, when we come to the question of interpretation that opinions differ most. This does not apply so much to *Daughter of France,* where no critics appear to disagree with V S-W's portrait of her subject; "she never presents Mademoiselle as anything but a goose," said Anthony Powell,[40] "and by the end one has a clear idea of just the sort of goose she was." Still less, of course, does it apply to *Pepita,* for it would be well-nigh impossible for anyone who had not known Lady Sackville to form an opinion of the justness of the portrait V S-W gives of her.

The book that gives rise to the greatest differences of opinion is *Saint Joan of Arc*. Here criticism is divided into two camps: one, the larger, accepts V S-W's interpretation of Saint Joan: the other disagrees with her on some aspect or other. To these must be added Sven Stolpe's vivid denunciation of the whole book.[41]

Contemporary criticism which was in agreement with the book spoke of "a new interpretation";[42] "Joan of Arc re-estimated".[43] The other camp took V S-W to task for a variety of reasons. We have already seen that her knowledge of the military methods and history of the fifteenth century was criticised. Another reviewer, apparently not noticing that he is using the word "attract" in two different senses, wonders why V S-W tries to "prove that Jeanne was 'unattractive', when we know that she attracted all France to her banner".[44]

Sven Stolpe dismisses V S-W's whole book with the words: "V. Sackville-Wests även på svenska utgivna biografi bör icke läsas; den är journalistiskt munvig, oinitierad och textkritiskt oskolad; dess hånfulla ton mot Anatole Frances lysande bok är närmast komisk."[45] His remarks about style need no comment here; they are amply answered

[35] Review of *Daughter of France* in *Mercure de France*, July 1959, p. 527.
[36] Supra, p. 88.
[37] Footnote 1 on p. 294 (Penguin edition), referring to *Bibl. Cotton Cleopatra.*
[38] The remark on p. 215 about Mlle's finances and V S-W's own.
[39] 8 May, 1959, p. 267.
[40] *Spectator,* 10 April, 1959, p. 518. More or less the same opinion is expressed by Peter Quennell in the *Observer,* 5 April, 1959, p. 21, and by the *Times Literary Supplement,* 8 May, 1959. p. 267.
[41] *Jeanne d'Arc,* Stockholm, 1949.
[42] *Times Literary Supplement,* 6 June, 1936, p. 469.
[43] *Manchester Guardian,* 10 July, 1936, p. 7.
[44] Edwin Muir in the *Scotsman,* 11 June, 1936.
[45] Stolpe, *op. cit., p. 382* ("V. Sackville-West's biography, which has also been published in Swedish, should not be read; it is journalistically glib, uninitiated and untrained in textual analysis: its scornful tone towards Anatole France's brilliant book is almost comical.")

elsewhere.[46] The crucial point for Stolpe appears to be the value V S-W places upon Anatole France's biography.[47] V S-W agrees entirely with Stolpe in his estimation of its literary worth; she refers to it as "a controversial, brilliant work, which may infuriate, but can never bore, the reader." She adds, however, "References as to sources of information unbelievably inaccurate; mistrust them all."[48] In passing, it may be noticed that Stolpe makes no mention of the reliability of France's book.[49]

In summing up what has been said about V S-W as a biographer, her two early works in the genre, *Aphra Behn* and *Andrew Marvell,* have not been taken into account; by reason of their briefness and their slighter nature, they are more to be reckoned as sketches than as biographies proper. If one considers her four major biographies, *Saint Joan of Arc, Pepita, The Eagle and the Dove* and *Daughter of France,* the following view seems to emerge.

She approaches her subject with an open and inquiring mind, untrammelled by preconceived ideas or theories. Her treatment is never unduly subjective, and the resulting portrait is historically true to the spirit and the facts known about the subject. A reservation must here be made concerning the historical background of *Saint Joan of Arc,* about her treatment of which criticism is not entirely in agreement. The biographies are extremely well and soberly written, and show a proper sense of responsibility towards subject and reader. There are, however, a few occasions on which the personality of the author distracts the reader's attention from the narrative. Each of her biographies produces an interpretation of the subject; an interpretation, moreover, which succeeds in convincing the reader of its correctness. This appears to be largely true even of the biographies that V S-W wrote of saints, although here her attitude to religious problems, which prevented her from accepting as self-evident many of the tenets which Catholics and others hold to be indisputable truth, undoubtedly resulted in some individuals being unable to find themselves in full agreement with her interpretation.

The conclusion seems inevitably to be that V S-W must be ranked as a biographer of distinction. If the occasional flaws to be found in her work exclude her from being reckoned among the very foremost, the interpretation she gives of her subjects, her openness of mind, the force of her good writing and her other merits make her a writer whose work will have to be taken into consideration by future biographers.

---

[46] See supra, pp. 87—8, 96.
[47] *La Vie de Jeanne d'Arc,* Paris, 1908.
[48] *Saint Joan of Arc,* p. 432.
[49] Later biographies of Jeanne d'Arc are of very little assistance in forming an opinion of the value of V S-W's book. The work published by Lucien Fabre, for example, *(Jeanne d'Arc,* Paris, 1947) contains neither index, bibliography, nor any reference to other works in the text. Joseph Calmette's book *(Jeanne d'Arc,* Paris, 1946) has no index or bibliography either, and references in the text are to French sources only. Jacques Cordier's *Jeanne d'Arc: sa personalité, son rôle* (Paris, 1948) has all three, but he mentions no untranslated English work at all except F. Lowell's American study of St. Joan from 1896 *(Joan of Arc,* Boston), about which he remarks: "Il est regrettable qu'elle n'ait pas été traduite en français." *(op. cit.,* p. 420). It seems legitimate to assume that Cordier does not read English and has not studied any of the later untranslated English works on Saint Joan, among which is V S-W's.

V. Sackville-West's Poetry

V S-W started writing poetry during the Georgian Era, and by 1922, when the fifth and last volume of E.M.'s *Georgian Poetry* appeared, she had already published two volumes of her own, *Poems of West and East,* 1917, and *Orchard and Vineyard,* 1921, in addition to the two she had had privately printed.

The term "Georgian poets" has, in the past, variously been used to describe those poets who wrote in the second decade of this century, to describe a poetic school, and, particularly in the years between the wars, as an uncritical term of abuse. In an admirable study of the period recently published, Robert Ross sums up the attitude that has frequently been adopted towards the Georgian poets in the following words:

> For some years the collective reputation of the Georgians has been at a low ebb. Indeed, perhaps no group of poets since the Pre-Raphaelites has suffered more, or more ignominiously, from the widespread acceptance of over-simplified stereotypes and critical half-truths, even among readers who should know better. Often the Georgians have been misrepresented because of the ignorance of their subsequent critics, but even more often they have been the victims of pure critical spleen. Many of the major Georgian poets surely deserve rescue from the almost universal obloquy which the weaknesses of a few of the brethren have drawn down upon the heads of the entire body.[1]

The Georgian revolt, which began about 1911, was "a part of the larger twentieth-century revolt against Humanism; in the beginning it was the poetic phase of a widespread revolt against Academism among all the arts; and, specifically in the field of poetry, it was a reaction against the dead hand of the Romantic-Victorian tradition."[2] In their revolt against the fin-de siècle æstheticism and sentimentality, the poets turned to the primitive, the brutal and the ugly.

This reaction against Victorianism soon divided into two main streams: one, which could accept neither the matter nor the manner of its predecessors: another, less radical, which was prepared to tolerate the matter, but was determined to find new ways of expressing it. The former was ready to trample on any convention in an effort to attain precision, and many of its members became Futurists, Vorticists, Imagists, etc., as well as espousing the cause of vers libre, with Ezra Pound as one of their foremost prophets. The latter stream was reluctant to sever all connections with the past and sought for truth to life through a new realism, though frequently retaining more traditional forms of verse.

[1] Robert H. Ross, *The Georgian Revolt: Rise and Fall of a Poetic Ideal, 1910—1922,* Southern Illinois University Press, 1965, p. ix.
[2] Ross, *op. cit.,* p. 22.

When Edward Marsh published the first two volumes of Georgian Poetry, in 1912 and 1915 respectively, he included a large number of vigorous poems written by the less revolutionary of these two streams. They were criticized by some reviewers for their "affected and self conscious brutality"[3] and for their rawness of tone, but for many poets and a large part of the reading public they were proof that poetry was at last undergoing a transformation. Beginning with the third volume, however, a change began to be noticeable. The old Georgians of volumes I and II began slowly to lose their dominance to Neo-Georgians, who increasingly began to set the tone of the later Georgian anthologies. "The Neo-Georgians were poets of the moon; their verse was washed white with the pale beams of Diana. Compared to the best of the Georgians the Neo-Georgians were pallid, lifeless, and monotonous. And they were to take Edward Marsh's anthology eventually from the real world of men and things, the world of truth to life, to an eternally moon-washed land of tropic nights."[4]

One of the newcomers in the fifth, and last, volume of Georgian Poetry, published in 1922, was V S-W, who contributed seven poems taken from Orchard and Vineyard.[5] They were not Neo-Georgian in character, but stood out by reason of their tone from much of the poetry included in the anthology. As Ross says, "with the striking exceptions of D.H. Lawrence's 'Snake', some selections from Blunden's The Shepherd and The Waggoner, and several from Vita Sackville-West's Orchard and Vineyard, Georgian Poetry V contained by and large the same kind of bloodless verse which had characterized Volume IV."[6]

> The difference in tone may be illustrated by "Full Moon":
> She was wearing the coral taffeta trousers
> Someone had brought her from Isfahan,
> And the little gold coat with pomegranate blossoms,
> And the coral-hafted feather fan;
> But she ran down a Kentish lane in the moonlight,
> And skipped in a pool of the moon as she ran.
>
> She cared not a rap for all the big planets,
> For Betelgeuse and Aldebaran,
> And all the big planets cared nothing for her.
> That small impertinent charlatan,
> As she climbed on a Kentish stile in the moonlight,
> And laughed at the sky through the sticks of her fan.[7]

The poet Herbert Palmer commented on this poem: "But Victoria Sackville-West's Full Moon (which appeared in the fifth Georgian anthology) is rather apart from her other work, and looks like a gesture of homage to the new school. ... A gesture of homage? But equally likely a gesture of derision: 'The small impertinent charlatan'. And it was the planets which were big and important rather than the moon. An odd, delightful, jaunty little lyric, which, in spite of its title Full Moon, does not really get the moonlight atmosphere of the new domination, and makes no particular bow to the Man in the Moon, whether that be J.C. Squire or a mere allegorical presence."[8]

[3] Times Literary Supplement, 27 February, 1913, p. 81.
[4] Ross, op. cit., p. 165.
[5] They were: "A Saxon Song", "Mariana in the North", "Full Moon", "Sailing Ships", "Trio", "Bitterness" and "Evening".
[6] Ross, op. cit., p. 212.
[7] Reprinted in Collected Poems, p. 258.
[8] Herbert Palmer, Post-Victorian Poetry, London, 1938, pp. 185—6.

Derisive? Probably. V S-W makes it clear in one of a series of radio talks she gave on modern poetry that "with the Georgians we are still in the company of poets who think that the poetic conventions are good enough for them; and who elect to retreat into the sanctified cloisters of the poetic paradise, taking their readers with them, rather than blunt the delicate weapons of their art against an enemy who does not play the game according to their rules."[9] Furthermore, her article on the future of the novel shows that she had little respect for mere competent mediocrity and imitativeness; her remark that the novel "is well done, certainly; but it is being done over and over and over again. Repetition is death"[10] would not apply with less force to poetry, where her critical standards were even higher.

Of the other poems by V S-W in *Georgian Poetry* V, Herbert Palmer states: "But if Blunden is shown at his most pastoral, Victoria Sackville-West is left a little more to surmise. One of her selected poems, *Bitterness,* is much more symbolical than is usual with Georgian poetry, and her frequent inclination to write of the passions and adventures of the human soul is somewhat at variance with her country-life aloofness."[11]

If V S-W was influenced by the Neo-Georgians, that influence was almost certainly a negative one. She does, however, owe a debt to the older Georgians and those of their successors who revolted against the sterility of poetic diction that was widespread in the second and third decades of this century. Her attitude is illustrated in the opening sentences of a talk on Wordsworth that she delivered in 1944 to the Royal Society of Literature. To bring out his relevance in relation to modern poetry, she began by making the assumption that he was born in 1907 instead of 1770, and went on: "He was thus of just the right age by 1930 to react vigorously against the so-called Georgian School of poets [by which she almost certainly meant the Neo-Georgians]. The attitude and idiom of this school appeared to him completely outworn and divorced from reality; and ... he proceeded boldly to outrage the accepted standards of taste and vocabulary; an attempt which met with little favour from the critics or the public, but which, considered in retrospect, can be seen now as setting up another milestone along the long road of English literature".[12]

From a poet who makes such a declaration one would naturally expect verse that is free from outworn poetic diction and is in close touch with reality. One of the characteristics of much of V S-W's poetry is, in fact, its freshness of imagery and diction, based on her keen powers of observation and originality. This applies particularly to her bucolic poetry, above all to *The Land* and *The Garden.*[13]

Contemporary poets seem to have influenced V S-W very little. T.S. Eliot, for example, early became for her almost an obsession, a symbol of pessimism and the negative outlook on life. Such was the strength of this antipathy, which seems to have been engendered by *The Waste Land,* that she was later unable to appreciate the Eliot who could offer rebirth through the death of self. In 1945, she could still write:

"April is the cruellest month, breeding
Lilacs out of the dead land, mixing
Memory and desire, stirring
Dull roots with spring rain."

---

[9] "Poetry of Today", *Radio Times,* 2 November, 1928, p. 290.
[10] "The Future of the Novel", *Week-end Review,* 18 October, 1930, p. 535.
[11] Palmer, *op. cit.,* p. 212.
[12] "Wordsworth: Especially in Relation to Modern Poetry", *Essays by Divers Hands,* XXII (1945), 100.
[13] For a brief analysis of the imagery in *The Garden,* see Stevens, *op. cit.,* pp. 34—40.

Would that my pen like a blue bayonet
Might skewer all such cats'-meat of defeat;
No buttoned foil, but killing blade in hand.
The land and not the waste land celebrate,
The rich and hopeful land, the solvent land,
Not some poor desert strewn with nibbled bones,
A land of death, sterility, and stones.[14]

If this was how V S-W regarded Eliot and those who worked in a similar spirit, then the only influence they could have exercised upon her would probably have been one of reaction, causing her to move even further away from everything they stood for. In view of the above, it seems not unlikely that the idea, and particularly the title, of *The Land,* which V S-W probably began writing in 1923, should be regarded, at least to some extent, as an answer to *The Waste Land* (1922).

Walter de la Mare appears to have been the only contemporary poet that V S-W singled out for praise. Her appreciation of him is clearly expressed in a lecture she read to the British Academy in 1953,[15] and in a radio tribute she broadcast on the occasion of his eightieth birthday that year.[16] V S-W undoubtedly admired de la Mare as a poet, but was she influenced by his work? A comparison of their poetry must yield the answer "not noticeably".

Among the remarks that V S-W made about de la Mare in the Wharton Lecture is one which merits particular consideration, for it might with equal justice have been used about V S-W herself:

He is far too original and personal a poet to derive from anbody; even, I would say, to be greatly influenced.[17]

One influence that is important when considering the work of V S-W is that of the Symbolists and Post-Symbolists. As early as 1926 she made it clear that she considered one of the gains to modern poetry was "a question of focus", which "was born in France where Mallarmé and Rimbaud, no less than Cézanne, began to see life from a queer, unfamiliar, oblique angle, something like a caricature, which surprises us first by its unlikeness, and then by its likeness, to the object."[18]

Nineteenth century Symbolism was a protest against the prevailing realism which sought to substitute scientific art for that based on lost religious values. "The Realists had no use for that belief in a superior world above the senses which has been familiar in Europe since Augustine absorbed the doctrines of Neo-Platonism; they had a stern conviction that what mattered was truth and that truth could be found empirically in this world. ... Against this scientific Realism the Symbolists protested, and their protest was mystical in that it was made on behalf of an ideal world which was, in their judgement, more real than that of the senses. It was not in any strict sense Christian."[19]

V S-W also resented the yoke of realism. In her article on the future of the novel, she complained that "circumstantial detail—once so exciting a discovery—frets us now, and irritates. We are bored by the aspidistra on the lodging-house window-sill and by the pattern on the lace curtains shutting out the sun. Realism itself has turned into a

[14] *The Garden,* p. 63.
[15] "Walter de la Mare and 'The Traveller'", *Proceedings of the British Academy* XXXIX (1953), 23—36 (Wharton Lecture).
[16] "The Personality of Walter de la Mare", *Listener,* IL (30 April, 1953), 711—2.
[17] *Wharton Lecture,* p. 31.
[18] "Some Tendencies of Modern English Poetry", *Essays by Divers Hands,* VII (1927), 46.
[19] Bowra, *The Heritage of Symbolism,* London, 1943, pp. 2—3.

private schoolboy's irreverent gesture rather apprehensively made under the nose of Lord Brentford."[20] She also believed that:

> There is another world that doubles this poor world,
> Where intimations like a source, a stream
> Sprung from a rock by bolt of vision cleft
> Crowd on the spirit in an hour too brief
> But in its stab, extreme.[21]

She also used symbols, both in her prose and in her poetry, for example, Olver's distorting mirror in *Grey Wethers,* or the symbol of the rose in *The Garden.*

The two extremes of poetry are instruction on the one hand and magic on the other. The Post-Symbolists, in contrast to some of the Symbolists, "accept the fact that words have meanings and that poetry must be understood." "But," as Maurice Bowra points out, "they have none the less kept to the magical view of it. They aim at moving hearts and stirring imaginations."[22] This is an outlook that V S-W shares with them. In her works, the magical is most evident in her novels, for example in *Grey Wethers, Seducers in Ecuador, Grand Canyon,* and in several of her short stories, particularly *Gottfried Künstler.*

Above all, however, V S-W was "a poet in a tradition,"[23] or as Jacques Vallette puts it, "Victoria Sackville-West est de ces poètes classiques nés à toutes les époques. ... Ses motifs sont la campagne de l'Angleterre, d'Amérique et d'Orient, prise en soi ou suscitant et soutenant la méditation; des portraits de personnages réels et imaginaires; des drames intérieurs personnels ou inventés. Par le lyrisme subjectif et par la poésie descriptive, elle se rattache à la tradition romantique."[24]

V S-W was fully aware of the fact that she was writing in a tradition regarded as obsolete by many people who "suffer from the delusion that the possibilities of bucolic poetry are dead."[25] In the poem *Sissinghurst,* she refers to herself as:

> A tired swimmer in the waves of time
> I throw my hands up: let the surface close:
> Sink down through centuries to another clime,
> And buried find the castle and the rose . . .
> And here, by birthright far from present fashion,
> As no disturber of the mirrored trance
> I move, and to the world above the waters
> Wave my incognisance.[26]

She has also referred to herself as "a damned out-moded poet."[27] This awareness was possibly responsible, to some extent at least, for the periods of depression from which she sometimes suffered[28] and may also be the explanation why inspiration fails to illuminate some of her less successful poems. On the other hand, this sense of belonging

---

[20] "The Future of the Novel", *Week-end Review,* 18 October, 1930, p. 535.
[21] *The Garden,* p. 89.
[22] Bowra, *op. cit.,* p. 220.
[23] Richard Church, "V. Sackville-West: A Poet in a Tradition", *Fortnightly,* CXLVIII (1940), 601.
[24] "Victoria Sackville-West", *Mercure de France,* 1—III—1949, pp. 423—4.
[25] Richard Church, *op. cit.,* p. 604.
[26] *Sissinghurst,* reprinted in *Collected Poems,* pp. 111—2.
[27] See Vallette, *op. cit.,* p. 428, and Church, *op. cit.,* p. 607.
[28] See supra, p. 74.

to a tradition was also the source of much of her great strength; it was so deeply in-grained in her that, when asked about how she had written *The Land,* she was able to reply, "I had not read the Georgics until half of my own poem had been written, and then a friend to whom I showed it spoke of the resemblance, so after that I read it.[29]

V S-W's affinity to tradition manifests itself in a variety of ways. It is apparent in her diction and vocabulary no less than in her choice of subject-matter and form. The style in which she chooses to write her poetry is a simple and clear one, and although these are fundamental qualities of her nature, the choice was probably deliberate. "Mais," comments Vallette, "si elle demande un vêtement à des formes régulières et consacrées, elle le porte en maître. Son vocabulaire, dans l'éloquence, puise aux sour-ces de Marlowe et de Shakespeare; il s'affermit de mots saxons dans les chants rusti-ques; il emprunte parfois au XVIIIe siècle pré-wordsworthien sa précision élégante, avec une liberté familière et confidentielle qui le soustrait au pastiche."[30] Other echoes of Shakespeare are constantly to be met with in her poetry, above all, perhaps, in metrical cadences which carry the mind direct to him. As regards form, she clearly also owes more than a little to Thomson, particularly as she began to write *The Land* with-out having read Virgil; and John Clare and Edward Thomas are her immediate pre-cursors.

If we turn to a consideration of individual poems, a remark made by Richard Church provides an excellent introduction. She is, he said, "another poet given to the explora-tion of solitude, to a private agony, and its assuagement in the delights of the soil."[31] The subjective lyricism which characterizes a number of her shorter poems up to and including 1933, the year in which she published *Collected Poems,* is frequently nakedly passionate, intensely personal, and filled with unrest.[32] "Elle dit la liberté de l'amour, la naissance et la mort de la passion, la résignation attendrie ou cynique, l'inquiétude captive, l'aspiration à s'évader de la chair."[33]

Given its head, this tendency towards the unleashing of violent emotions might have led, and in some of her unpublished poems did lead, to excesses detrimental to the quality of her poetry. What saved her in the nineteen-twenties was probably the strength of tradition and the fact that she wrote *The Land.* In later years, she turned to religious speculation and wrote biographies, both of which may have had a steadying influence on her style.

The Land was in several respects a turning point in her poetic career. In deciding to write this long poem she was, at the same time, making a decision to subject herself to a discipline more rigorous than had been necessary for any of her shorter poems. A work on the scale of *The Land* demanded an objectivity, a precision, and a degree of planning far in excess of anything she had hitherto been compelled to employ. There can be little doubt that she gained immensely by having to do so.

To head the completed poem, V S-W chose two lines from *The Georgics:*

Nec sum animi dubius, verbis ea vincere magnum
quam sit et angustis hunc addere rebus honorem.[34]

Commenting on her choice of a heading, Richard Church says: "Through that restriction of theme, however, she has mastered more than her subject. She has mastered also

[29] Interview published in the *Lady,* 6 June, 1929, p. 771.
[30] Vallette, *op. cit.,* p. 425.
[31] Church, *op. cit.,* p. 601.
[32] They are the poems gathered under the headings "Love" and "King's Daughter" on pages 283—325 of *Collected Poems.*
[33] Vallette, *op. cit.,* p. 424.
[34] iii, 289—90.

the waywardness and turbulence of her moods, brought down their vagueness to a precision that is hard and objective, given them a universal out of a personal value. She has put her hand to the plough in more senses than one. She says that 'the country habit has me by the heart',[35] and her heart, under that discipline, works the more harmoniously with her mind. This process, a hard one which cannot be mastered merely by willing, needs time, patience and experience before it can be acquired. Once acquired, however, it produces that essential poetry which is content with simple words, unliterary associations, and humble effects."[36]

In the middle of the nineteen-thirties, when her thoughts began to turn to religious speculation, V S-W abandoned novel writing for a form that again required rigid discipline, namely biography. The need once more to marshal her thoughts and govern her emotions must have been an exercise that was beneficial to her poetry too, for her last poems, *Solitude* (1938) and *The Garden* (1946) show a control that was absent in some of her previous works.

The Land and *The Garden* are the two poems on which V S-W is most likely to be judged by posterity. *The Land* has almost a double validity for, apart from its poetic worth, it is a record of a rural culture that has governed the lives of a great number of Englishmen for several hundred years, but which was already fast disappearing when she wrote the poem. L.A.G. Strong recollects that he "heard farmers discussing Miss Sackville-West's long poem *The Land,* not as poetry, but as a manual of country matters. This in itself would be no commendation ... but, taken in conjunction with the fact that *The Land* was immediately acclaimed by poets, it means a great deal."[37] It is, however, with its poetic value that we are here concerned, and about this there can be little doubt. On its first apperance it was hailed with almost universal approval by the critics, the one notable exception being Edith Sitwell, who, replying to a statement by John Drinkwater that *The Land* contained some of the loveliest verse written in this century, retorted: "Well, *I* can only say that it does *not.* I am told by competent persons that Miss Sackville-West's prose is charming. It seems, therefore, a distinct pity to put it into metre. The book would probably be of great use to prospective farmers, for it is one long catalogue of agricultural implements, and the right way to do everything, —to 'stook' (whatever that may mean), and to thatch. The book tells you exactly when and how to reap and cut everything that grows. It also mentions birds' nests and Helen's breast."[38] However, when Edith Sitwell published her anthology of verse, *The Atlantic Book of British and American Poetry,* in 1958, it contained a five-page-long extract from *The Land*[39]—only one page less than she devoted to Thomas Hardy, and considerably more than was allotted to Emerson, Housman or D.H. Lawrence. The extract included a reference to birds' nests and to Helen's breast.

Subsequent criticism has confirmed the view of the first reviewers. L.A.G. Strong makes a point that had long needed stressing when he writes that "Blunden and another poet, V. Sackville-West, between them rescued English Nature poetry from the Georgians and restored it to its place."[40] Due partly to the indiscriminate manner in which the term had been used, several writers, while acknowledging the worth of the poem,[41] had classified *The Land* as Georgian Poetry, which it is not.

[35] *The Land,* p. 5.
[36] Church, *op. cit.,* p. 605.
[37] "English Poetry since Brooke", *The Nineteenth Century and After,* CXVI (1934), 464.
[38] *Cassell's Weekly,* 19 March, 1927.
[39] Pp. 832—6, (from *The Land,* pp. 50—7.)
[40] *Op. cit.,* p. 464.
[41] Among others, Herbert Palmer in *Post-Victorian Poetry,* London, 1938, pp. 278—9, and Geoffrey Bullough in *The Trend of Modern Poetry,* Edinburgh and London, 1949, pp. 69—70.

Grierson and Smith emphasize another aspect of the poem. "There is," they point out, "no false pastoralism about the pictures, nor yet the bitter realism of Crabbe: the land is a hard task-mistress, but a just one. *The Land* (1926) is a refreshing poem, more like Hesiod perhaps than Virgil, with something of the eighteenth century in its cool good sense."[42]

Richard Church's opinion is quite clear: "During the war I wrote a critical essay in the Fortnightly Review, which was then collected into book form . . . and published by Dents under the title EIGHT FOR IMMORTALITY. . . . As the title suggests my view of her poetry is that it is in the permanent tradition and is likely to endure the criticism of time when more fashionable verse has been forgotten."[43] With this opinion Jacques Vallette would probably have concurred, for he wrote in his article on V S-W: "Eliot, puis Auden, Spender, MacNeice, Day Lewis, D. Thomas et tous ceux des années trente et suivantes ont ajouté des chapitres glorieux à la poésie anglaise. D'autres, dans le même temps, exploitaient d'autres domaines dans des formes empruntées au passé. Ils ne paraissent pas avoir été mis à leur rang jusqu'ici. Le temps est venu de le faire: après une vague de nouveautés, d'ailleurs valables et fécondes, le roc de la tradition émerge: ce qui reste ne date pas."[44]

The Garden has received much less critical attention than *The Land*. In part this is probably due to the fact that V S-W died just about the time when second thoughts about the poem might have been expected. Partly, perhaps, it may be that critics felt as a lack what V S-W herself experienced as a difficulty when she was writing the poem. "It is much more difficult than *The Land,* because the inherent dignity of agriculture is lacking, and seed-boxes are not so romantic as tilth."[45] And partly it may be because it is, by reason of the underlying speculation on religion and death, a far more personal poem than *The Land,* and it is therefore much more difficult to form an impartial opinion of it. Whatever the reason, *The Garden,* which was very well received on publication, has not shown the same ability as *The Land* to capture the imagination of the public; it has not yet been reprinted, although the first edition of 15,000 copies sold out in September 1961.[46] It remains to be seen how future critics will judge this long poem in the English tradition in which "never stretching thought or language beyond the range which comes to her naturally, she accomplishes a quiet perfection from restrained poetic speech which is likely to be listened to after louder and more singular voices have wearied their audience."[47]

[42] Herbert Grierson and J.C. Smith, *A Critical History of English Poetry,* London, 1944, p. 505.
[43] Letter dated 18 June, 1971, from Richard Church to the present author.
[44] *Op. cit.,* p. 423.
[45] *Diaries and Letters, 1939—45,* p. 265.
[46] Letter dated 26 November, 1970, from Michael Joseph Ltd. to the present author.
[47] *Times Literary Supplement,* 15 June, 1946, p. 285.

Conclusion

It must be very rare for a poet of renown also to be a distinguished biographer as well as a good novelist. V S-W was all three. She also wrote books on gardening, about which her knowledge was impressive, which may be, and are, read for the sheer pleasure of reading them. The foreword to the German translation of one of these books remarks "daß die starke dichterische Ader der Autorin, ihre Originalität und ihr Humor durch alle ernsthafte Pflanzenkenntnis und genaue Naturbeobachtung immer wieder durchbrechen, so daß eine schöne Einheit entsteht."[1]

V S-W was never a professional author in the sense that she wrote in order to earn her daily bread. With the possible exception of the years between 1930 and 1936 she had no need to do so. The principal reason why she wrote was certainly the creative urge common to all artists, but in part it seems also to have been due to an inner compulsion to set down on paper in some transmuted form the problems and doubts which beset her. V S-W's acute consciousness of her mixed ancestry, her upbringing under her mother, her difficulty in establishing contact with people and other factors produced a duality in her nature which she does not seem to have overcome until she was over fifty years of age. Later in life, partly perhaps through the influence of her sister-in-law, but possibly also afflicted with *Angst,* her thoughts turned to religion, in which she sought, not consolation, but an explanation of the contradictions in life she could not but notice around her. She would have wished to be granted faith, the ability to believe wholeheartedly in Christianity or some other religion, but there is no evidence that such faith ever came to her.

She therefore resorted to an artistic medium in order to explain her difficulties to herself, and the result was literature, both in prose and poetry, which has won international recognition.

The above should not for a moment be taken to imply that an inner compulsion arising out of personal problems was the sole source of her inspiration, although it may well have played a considerable part in some of her writing. The best of her work, both in poetry and in prose, owes far more to her native originality, a sense of the traditions of literature, psychological insight, an acute power of observation, a natural gift of style and a feeling for language. When she had learnt to discipline her turbulent emotions, which she did by forcing herself to work within a rigidly fixed scheme, she was able to write works of great power and simplicity, such as *The Land*.

If anyone were to ask why the life and works of V S-W are worth studying, the answer would be that it is because she was a particular sort of person who lived at a par-

---

[1] *Aus meinem Garten,* Heimeran-Verlag, München, 1966, p. 7.

ticular moment in time. By an accident of birth, she belonged to a class many members of which were not able to take part in the social struggle that was rife in Europe. The detachment this gave her renders her free from a sense of urgency, and she was little influenced by the sound and fury around her. It also enabled her to keep her eyes fixed on the eternal values that her feeling for tradition told her were the essential ones, for, as she has said, she felt "a lack of interest in what must always be temporary things, things that in a thousand years' time will have become meaningless,"[2] This is why she could also say "neither do I feel attracted to *la poésie engagée*".[3] It becomes dated all too soon.

This detachment, however, did not mean that she did not observe. She both observed and recorded, and the record is the more valuable for the detachment. There can be little doubt that V S-W regarded many of the phenomena of modern life with distaste; her private correspondence bears witness to that. But in her art she never condemns any but her peers.

To her art V S-W brought a real poetic gift. But, like all true artists, her attitude towards her muse was one of great humility. "You know," she wrote to H.N., "I do get so frightfully, frenziedly excited writing poetry. It is the only thing that makes me truly and completely happy. And then I feel that what I have been writing is so very poor— so wretched a reflection of what has been going on in my mind while I am at it. Why should one rise so high and then go so completely flop?"[4]

V S-W's detachment and her observation from a unique point of view, her independence and the fact that she is little influenced by passing literary fashions, her sense of tradition and her eye for eternal values, the gift of poetic speech with which to express her sentiments, and her humility towards her art: these are the reasons why V S-W is worth studying.

---

[2] *Diaries and Letters, 1945—62*, p. 38.
[3] Vallette, *op. cit.*, in an unpublished letter he quotes on p. 427.
[4] *Diaries and Letters, 1945—62*, p. 38.

Knole from the air.

An estimate of the reliability of the information contained in *Pepita,* Part 2

Almost the only sources of much of the information about V S-W's early life are *Pepita* and the MS Autobiography of 1920[1], that is to say, information that she herself provides. It is frequently impossible to check her statements against a secondary source. It therefore seems desirable to be able to form an estimate of the accuracy with which V S-W writes on biographical and historical subjects, particularly as her childhood experiences were clearly of great importance to the development of her personality and writing.

Although many of V S-W's statements cannot be checked, it is, perhaps, possible to provide what courts of law refer to as "evidence of character"; if an examination of similar works she had written previous to *Pepita* show integrity and accuracy, then it would be reasonable to assume that *Pepita* is also reliable.

Prior to 1937, V S-W had written one historical survey, *(Knole and the Sackvilles)* two biographical sketches *(Aphra Behn* and *Andrew Marvell*[2]*)* and one full-length biography *(Saint Joan of Arc*[3]*).* The accuracy of *Knole and the Sackvilles* can be checked with comparative ease against *Burke's Peerage and Baronetage, D.N.B.,* Phillips, *op. cit.,* Bacquet, *op. cit.,* and standard works of reference. While she was writing the book she had an opportunity of studying a trained biographer at work, for Charles Phillips, who spent the years 1913 to 1922 doing the research work necessary for his two-volume history of the Sackville family[4], showed V S-W "large lumps of his manuscript somewhat illegibly hand-written on foolscap paper."[5]

Bacquet quotes from or refers to *Knole and the Sackvilles* twenty-five times in his work on Thomas Sackville. On one occasion he expresses uncertainty about her objectivity in saying that "Fillsack" (Sir Richard) Sackville appears not to have been griping or penurious;[6] on another he disagrees with V S-W's interpretation of "29 Ann.

---

[1] This MS Autobiography, which occupies seventy-two pages of a folio notebook, was written at a time of crisis in her life (see supra, p. 32). She wrote it "urged by the necessity of truth telling" (MS Autobiography, p. 1), obviously in order to clear her own mind about her situation, and adds. "Having written it down, I shall be able to trust no one to read it." *(Ibid.,* p. 1). As it was not written for publication and is extremely frank .there seems no reason to doubt its accuracy, more particularly as those facts which can be checked invariably prove correct. It is interesting to note, however, that she gave pseudonyms to all the people who figure in it. The MS Autobiography and a typed copy of it are in the possession of Mr Nigel Nicolson, at Sissinghurst Castle. All references in this dissertation are to the typed copy.

[2] Gerald Howe, London, 1927, and Faber & Faber, London, 1929 respectively.

[3] Cobden, Sanderson, London, 1936.

[4] Phillips, *op. cit.,* I, ix.

[5] *Knole and the Sackvilles,* p. v.

[6] Bacquet, *op. cit.,* p. 20, footnote 48.

etc."[7] The majority of his references to V S-W's book are, however, either for confirmation of what he states, or as one of his sources.[8] A reading of Phillips, *op. cit.* and the other works mentioned above has not revealed any discrepancy between their facts and hers.[9]

Saint Joan of Arc was a major work calling for historical accuracy, objectivity, and a good sense of balance, for "anything new that a writer can now hope to put into a study of Saint Joan of Arc must, it seems, be in the way of interpretation. ... It is ... not probable that any further material of importance will be found."[10]

With one reservation,[11] informed literary criticism is clearly of the opinion that the work has integrity and is accurate. The *Times Literary Supplement* praises her restraint:

> It appears that she has deliberately set herself to avoid emotion and to write in a sober, even at times a pedestrian, strain. The effect is at first a little disappointing, but as we settle down to a book which it is very difficult to stop reading we appreciate more and more the biographer's method. Not only are the events narrated with admirable clarity; the portrait that emerges is as impressive as it is satisfactory and the speculation intelligent, if cautious.[12]

Regarding her open approach and the way in which she arrives at her conclusions, Basil de Selincourt comments:

> Miss Sackville-West, moreover, has no anxiety to impose her own interpretations, and, as far as she can, lets the reader see her conclusions in the process of formation by generous quotation from the original texts.[13]

The *Church Times,* finally, is of the opinion that it is:

> more than a good book; it is scholarly. The author has solved the problem quite sucessfully by using authorities without pedantry. She quotes a good deal, and summarizes a great deal more. But she has picked out the right passages to quote; they have a real bearing and a profound interest; and she summarizes, without writing into the narrative slabs of imaginative nonsense evolved from her own inner self-consciousness.[14]

Pepita is in two parts. The first part, dealing mainly with the lives of Pepita herself and V S-W's grandfather, is based on the voluminous evidence collected by lawyers between 1896 and 1910 as material for the lawsuit to decide the succession to the Sackville title.[15] V S-W herself says: "I should like to explain here that nothing in the following pages is either invented or even embellished. Down to the smallest, the very smallest particular, it is all absolutely and strictly true."[16] Considerations of time have made it impossible for the present author to check in detail this vast amount of material. Spot checks, however, revealed no discrepancy, or gave any cause to doubt V S-W's assertion.

In view of the above, it therefore seems reasonable to assume that those objective facts in the second part of *Pepita* which cannot be checked against secondary sources are probably correct. The subjective information and opinions expressed by V S-W in the book are of value in interpreting her attitude to her surroundings, and their accuracy is of secondary importance.

[7] *Ibid.,* p. 25, footnote 80.
[8] *Ibid.,* p. 359.
[9] See, however, the error detected in *Burke's Peerage* (supra, p. 13, note 8.)
[10] *Times Literary Supplement,* 6 June, 1936, p. 469.
[11] See supra, p. 94.
[12] 6 June, 1936, p. 469.
[13] *Observer,* 7 June, 1936.
[14] 1 June, 1936.
[15] *Pepita,* pp. 14—5.
[16] *Ibid.,* p. 14.

A Question of Inspiration

The other day we received the following letter from a correspondent:

Sir,—In Clifford Dyment's new book, *Poems 1935—1948,* there is included the following poem:

SAINT AUGUSTINE AT 32

Girl, why do you follow me
When I come to the threshold of the holy place?
My resolution falters: it seems a death to enter
When, turning back, I look into your face.
I saw you when I lay alone
And ran from you as from a searching light
Into the gentle, acquiescent
Obscurity of the night.
I crave communion that is not words
And life fulfilled in my cell alone—
And you, you come with your lips and your gold hair
And at your feet is a leaf that the wind has blown.

The lines struck me as familiar. I turned up the *Poetry Review* of June—July, 1949, and there read:

THE NOVICE TO HER LOVER

Why must you follow me
When I come to the threshold of this holy place?
My resolution falters and it seems death to enter
When, turning back, I look upon your face.
I could renounce you when I lay alone;
I ran from you as from a hungry light
Into the gentle, the infinite, the healing
Clemency of the night.
I crave an eloquence that is not words,
I seek fulfilment in the kiss of stone—
But you, you come with your mouth and your dark hair
And at your feet a leaf that the wind has blown.

V. Sackville-West

In Mr. Dyment's book his poem is dated 1944. I therefore consulted his 1944 volume, *The Axe In The Wood,* and there found the poem in a version even nearer Miss Sackville-West's. The mystery of the parallel between the two poems has puzzled me. I am unable to find any explanation. Can any of your readers?

Leonard Hickman

Clearly, Mr. Hickman raised a fascinating question. But perhaps there was a simple explanation—for instance, that both Mr. Dyment and Miss Sackville-West had, unknown to each other, adapted or translated some earlier poem. So, before printing Mr. Hickman's letter, we decided to send a copy to the poets themselves.

From Mr. Dyment we had this reply:

Yes, I have heard about the extraordinarily puzzling similarity between the two poems, as Miss Sackville-West herself wrote to me about it. I am as mystified as she is. All I know is that my poem was first published in January, 1943, in the *St. Martins' Review* and subsequently reprinted in book form in 1944 and 1949, and that it is not a translation. I think it would be very interesting if Mr. Hickman's letter were published, as it might bring forward other cases of the same sort of thing. It's all very odd.

And from Miss Sackville-West:

The facts, so far as I am concerned, are:

(a) I wrote my poem *The Novice to her Lover* some time in 1942 or early in 1943, when I was engaged on an essay* about St. Thérèse of Lisieux, the "novice" I had in mind. I put the poem away and thought no more about it. I did not even get it typed, and no one saw it except one person, to whom, as a recently converted Catholic and a devotee of St. Thérèse, I sent it embodied in a letter. I have now made inquiries from this person, who assures me that she neither showed the poem to anyone, nor caused any copy of it to be made. Thus, no one but myself and this one other person had seen my poem, until—

(b) The *Poetry Review* wrote to ask me for some unpublished verses of mine for their Jubilee numbers in the summer of 1949. I then looked through my MSS. Book; I found this poem; and they duly printed it.

(c) In November, 1949, I borrowed a copy of Mr. Dyment's *Poems,* published by Messrs. Dent, and therein read with some astonishment a poem which I recognised as almost identical with a poem of my own.

(d) I then immediately wrote to Mr. Dyment who, I felt, must be as puzzled as I. He agreed that he was; but reminded me of a letter I had written him in 1944, in reference to his book of poems entitled *The Axe in the Wood,* of which he had sent me a copy through his publishers, Messrs. Dent, and in which his poem *St. Augustine at 32* was included. It seems that in my letter to Mr. Dyment I singled out this poem for especial praise. The whole story becomes less and less explicable.

Why did I not recognise my own poem in Mr. Dyment's volume in 1944?

Why did I recognise it at once in Mr. Dyment's volume in 1949?

How did Mr. Dyment and I come to write the same poem, in a rather unusual metre, about two very different saints, at approximately the same time, i.e. 1942 or 1943?

It is of course, unthinkable that either I or Mr. Dyment should have "lifted" a poem from one another. That supposition can be dismissed. But what, then, is the explanation?

I have none to offer.

---

* Published in *The Eagle and the Dove,* 1943.

Have our readers any explanation? Or knowledge of any similar instances of the same inspiration visiting two poets?

And what if all of animated nature
Be but organic Harps diversely fram'd,
That tremble into thought, as o'er them sweep
Plastic and vast, one intellectual breeze . . .

Is this an illustration of the poet acting, as Coleridge believed he might, as an Aeolian harp? Or is there a less romantic explanation, such as a common source in some book of memoirs or devotions which both poets had read and both forgotten?

From the *New Statesman and Nation,* 21 January, 1950, p. 62.

Unpublished Poems by V. Sackville-West

In December 1963 the present author visited Sissinghurst Castle and was allowed to spend several days in V S-W's study in the tower examining the papers which, according to Mr Nigel Nicolson, no one had touched up to that time. On the writing desk and in brief-cases and files around and under it were the first and second drafts of *The Garden,* the first or second drafts of eighty-three published poems and the drafts of one hundred and ninety-seven unpublished poems, as well as a number of brief prose drafts on various subjects. From this copious material the following unpublished poems have been selected to illustrate some facets of V S-W's personality.

Contact with beauty, for me, is direct and immediate.
The sight of beauty, for me, is the meaning of beauty.
I do not get the meaning at a second remove.
An ocean, a landscape, or a lovely woman
Are immediate and complete experiences.
A tree in winter, bare, without the loveliness
Of leaves, a tree bare to its branches
Lovelier far than dressed in summer beauty.
I like things stripped down to truth,
Un-prettied, unromanticised.

DIARY POEM

My heart is broken against grey stone,
Against the Kentish Rag.
Smashed against it as ships in wreck
Smash on a Cornish crag.

Cracked is my heart and cannot mend;
It broke twelve years ago;
Never, never, never again
Shall I call my heart my own.

My heart was torn from my broken breast
And thrown against the stone—
The stone of my own friendly home
That broke it in the end.

Never, never, never to mend;
A smash that never heals;
Oh sorrow, that the thing I love
Should be the thing that kills.

Knole, you would not have broken me?
Me, passionate and wild?
You loved me, surely, in so far
As stone can love its child?

Knole, when I went from you, you missed
One of your many children, specially?
God knows I gave you all my love, my agony,
Scarcely a stone of you I had not kissed.

Knole! Knole! I stretch my hands to you in prayer,
You, grey and solid; you, enduring, staid;
You do not know what surges beat against your walls;
Miss me a little, I who am your soul.

DIARY POEM

I look at my name on an envelope:
The Hon. Mrs Harold Nicolson
In beautiful legal type
From my solicitor's office
Enclosing a legal form
For the purchase of land in Kent.

Then I look at my other name,
My own my personal name,
The name my ancestors gave to me,
The name I have kept for myself.

And it seems to me that the name I bore
Is better adapted to lands in Kent
Than the Scottish name my sons must bear,
For my son has gone to the Western Isles,
My son has gone to the Hebrides,[1]
My son doesn't give a damn for Kent,
But I was bred from Sussex and Kent,
And my name is dear to me.

[1] Mr Nigel Nicolson bought the Shiant Islands in the Outer Hebrides in 1937 (see *Diaries and Letters, 1930—39*, p. 288).

I will hold to my own, old name,
Walled within walls of Knole;
I will not sink my pride, my soul,
In another's pride and fame.

I have pride enough of my own, thank ·God,
And I have earned my right
To be no tin can on another's tail,—
Rattle, and dragged about.

My proudest boast: I will give my love
Stintless, with all its pain;
But my name is mine, and my lands in Kent
Should be mine, like my books, in name.

HEREDITY

What is this thing, this bond,
That brings us here together?
That keeps us, though we roam,
All on a length of tether?

Why are our faces cut
All in the same sad feature?
It is a quirk, a trick
Played on us all by Nature.

I am not you, I am I;
Nothing is foreordained.
I hold my liberty
Unstained and unconstrained.

Because I have your eyes
Does it mean I have your heart?
No, you are you, I am I,
Independent and apart.

Violently I refuse
All seisin with another,
Be she my kinswoman,
Be he my own blood-brother.

—Yet stay. Had he that lies
Dead in the chapel, not
The same unhappy eyes?
My father, that me begot?

Yet stay. Have they not all,
The portraits in gilded frame,
Upstairs, the same sad pensive look
The same, and still the same?

What is this thing, this strain,
Persistent, what this shape
That cuts us from our birth,
And seals without escape?

Long Barn, 16 February, 1928

I suppose other people endure the same dissatisfactions—
I suppose they all think that nobody understands them;
I suppose they think that words are no good, and that anyway
        one can never say what one means.
That is where sex comes in, the arch-deceiver.
Sex deludes one into the belief that one has attained real
        contact with another person;
And since the horrible loneliness of the soul makes one
        crave for some contact,
One turns gratefully to sex as a short-cut to contact.
But it isn't true, it isn't true; yet what is true?
Is it true, ever, to say "I love!" with its implications,
Knowing that the truth wears quite a different face for oneself
        or another?
Yes, it may be true to say "I love", but in the last resort
There is no possibility of contact, except in a brief delusion.

Is it true, ever true, to say "I love"?
Yes, it can, I believe, be true.
It is true when the concerns of other people matter to me
        more than my own concerns,
When there is no selfishness involved.
When I mind, vitally, in myself, if they are cold or warm,
Whether they catch their train or have to linger on platforms;
Whether they meet with applause or a snub in their undertakings;
If these things matter, then, in my innermost self
As though they affected myself, then I know I love.

117

I am the snail
    crawling out at night to devour the flower.
I am the flower devoured by the snail—
I am the lion in his desert
I am the gazelle brought down by the lion—
I am the dog who lies down by man's hearth.

I am the horse—who was once no bigger than a hare
    but who now pulls men's carriages and farm-waggons.
I have grown to the Suffolk Punch and the Percheron—
I am the man
I am the star—the black dwarf
I am the Galaxy
I am the speed of light
I am the atom. I am the atom bomb.
I am the Universe, receding so fast that no telescope
    can catch up with it
I AM because I think I am.

And now my dog comes and pokes me with his nose, saying it's time for me to have my dinner.

And; so it ends.
We who were lovers may be friends.
I have some weeks in which to steel
My heart and teach myself to feel
Only a sober tenderness
Where once was passion's loveliness.

I had not thought that there would come
Your touch to make our music dumb,
Your meeting touch upon the string
That still was vibrant, still could sing
When I impatiently ~~might~~ wait
Or parted from you at the gate.

You took me weak and unprepared.
I had not thought that you who shared
My days, my nights, my heart, my life,
Would slash me with a naked knife
And gently tell me not to bleed
But to accept your crazy creed.

You speak of God, but you have cut
The one last thread, as you have shut
The one last door that open stood
To show me still the way to God.
If this be God, this pain, this evil,
I'd sooner change and try the Devil.

Darling, I thought of nothing mean;
I thought of killing straight and clean.
You're safe; that's gone, that wild caprice,
But tell me once before I cease,
Which does your Church esteem the kinder role,
To kill the body, or destroy the soul?

The Published Works of V. Sackville-West

POETRY

Work	Reprinted in
Chatterton: A Drama in Three Acts, J. Salmon, Sevenoaks, 1909. (Privately printed).	
"The Dancing Elf", *The English Review,* XV (August 1913).	*Poems of West and East.*
Constantinople, Complete Press, London, 1915. (Privately printed).	*Poems of West and East.*
Poems of West and East, John Lane, London, 1917.	*Collected Poems.*
"Ad Astra", *The Anglo-French Review,* III (June 1920), 468—9.	*Orchard and Vineyard.*
"Escape", *The Anglo-French Review,* III (June 1920), 496.	*Orchard and Vineyard.*
"A Fallen Soldier", *Observer,* 5 June, 1921.	*Orchard and Vineyard.*
"Sorrow of Departure", *Observer,* 5 June, 1921.	*Orchard and Vineyard.*
"Evening", London *Mercury,* IV (September 1921), 467.	*Orchard and Vineyard.*
Orchard and Vineyard, John Lane, London, 1921.	*Collected Poems.*
"Winter Song", London *Mercury,* VII (December 1922), 128—9.	*The Land.*
"Alice Meynell", *Observer,* 17 December, 1922.	*Collected Poems.*
"Moonlight", London *Mercury,* VIII (May 1923).	
"Song", London *Mercury,* VIII (May 1923).	*Collected Poems.*
"Song", London *Mercury,* VIII (May 1923).	
"Making Cider", London *Mercury,* VIII (October 1923), 567.	*The Land.*
"The Bee-Master", London *Mercury,* VIII (Oct. 1923), 568—70.	*The Land.*
"Sea Sonnet", *Poetry Review,* VIII (Dec. 1923).	*Collected Poems.*
"Tuscany", London *Mercury,* IX (March 1924), 461—2.	*The Land.*
"The Island", *Nation and Athenaeum,* XXXVI (March 1925), 776.	*The Land.*
"Woodcraft", London *Mercury,* XI (April 1925).	*The Land.*
"On the Lake", *Nation and Athenaeum,* XXXVIII (December 1925), 469.	*Collected Poems.*
The Land, William Heinemann, London, 1926.	*Collected Poems.*
"Winter", *New Paths on Helicon,* Th. Nelson, London, 1927.	
"Black Tarn", London *Mercury,* XV (March 1927).	*Collected Poems.*
"At Rhey", *Bermondsey Book,* IV, (June 1927).	*Collected Poems.*
"In Syria", *Literary Digest,* XCV (October 1927), N.Y.	*Collected Poems.*
"Palmyra", *Time and Tide,* IX (17 February, 1928).	*Collected Poems.*
"Love Song", *Time and Tide,* IX (9 March, 1928), 224.	*Collected Poems.*
"Eclipse", *Daily Express,* 27 July, 1928.	
"Bowl of Blue Beads", *Daily Express,* 22 October, 1928.	*Collected Poems.*
"Idyll", *Time and Tide,* X (10 March, 1929).	*King's Daughter.*
"Nocturne", *Listener,* I (13 March, 1929), 327.	
"Illusions", London *Mercury,* XX (October 1929), 556.	*King's Daughter.*

King's Daughter, Hogarth Press, London, 1929.   Collected Poems.
"Poem", Time and Tide, X (8 November, 1929), 1338.
"Storm in the Mountains", London Mercury, XXI (December
  1929).   Collected Poems.
"Peace in the Mountains", Poetry Review, XXI (January 1930).   Collected Poems.
"Persia", Spectator, CXLVI (31 January, 1931).   Collected Poems.
"Chanson Perpetuelle", Listener, V (10 June, 1931), 981.   Collected Poems.
Rilke, Duineser Elegien, trans. (with Edward Sackville-West),
  Hogarth Press, London, 1931.
Sissinghurst, Hogarth Press, London, 1931.   Collected Poems.
Invitation to Cast out Care, Faber & Faber, London, 1931.   Collected Poems.
"Reddín", A Miscellany of Verse Never Before Published,
  Victor Gollancz, London, 1931.   Collected Poems.
"A Dream", Week-end Review, IV (5 December, 1931).   Collected Poems.
"Encounter", Week-end Review, V (5 January, 1932).   Collected Poems.
"Absence", Week-end Review, V (26 March, 1932).   Collected Poems.
"The Bull", Week-end Review, VI (1 October, 1932).   Collected Poems.
"To any M.F.H.", Review of Reviews, LXXXV (January 1933).   Collected Poems.
Collected Poems, Hogarth Press, London, 1933, Doubleday,
  Doran, N.Y. 1934.
"December Night", New Statesman and Nation, XII (5 Decem-
  ber, 1936), 892—3.
Solitude, Hogarth Press, London, 1938, Doubleday, Doran,
  N.Y., 1939.
"Winter Afternoon", Times Literary Supplement, 5 November,
  1938.
"Reminiscence", Listener, XXI (23 March, 1939).
"Gas-Proof Room, New Statesman and Nation, XVIII (2 De-
  cember, 1939).
"Prayer in the Desert", Observer, 10 December, 1939.
"Appeal", St. Martin's Review, March 1940.
"Personal Valour", Observer, 23 June, 1940.
"July, 1940", Observer, 21 July, 1940.
"In Memoriam: Virginia Woolf," Observer, 6 April, 1941.
Selected Poems, Hogarth Press, London, 1941.
"August, 1941", Observer, 24 August, 1941.
"The Comet", Times Literary Supplement, 17 April, 1943.
"On a Dutch Flower Picture", Spectator, CLXXI (31 Decem-
  ber, 1943).   The Garden.
"Blast", Observer, 23 April, 1944.
"Ethel Smythe", Observer, 14 May, 1944.
"Spitfire and Flying Bomb", Observer, 25 June, 1944.
"Les Français parlent aux Français", Times Literary Supple-
  ment, 15 July, 1944.
"This War Will Soon Be Over", Observer, 14 May, 1944.   The Garden.
"The Crater in the Field", Country Life, XCVI (8 Sept., 1944).   The Garden.
"Searchlights", Times Literary Supplement, 16 September, 1944.   The Garden.
"Blackout", Observer, 8 October, 1944.   The Garden.
"Dog", Country Life, XCVI (27 October, 1944).
"Stone Manger", Times Literary Supplement, 23 Dec., 1944,
  p. 620.   The Garden.
"Nativity", New Statesman and Nation, XXX (22 December,
  1945).   The Garden.
"You Happy Baby at the Cottage Door", Decachord, XXIII
  (January—February 1946).
The Garden, Michael Joseph, London, Doubleday, New York,
  1946.
"Ellen Terry", London Times, 27 February, 1947.
"The Novice to her Lover", Poetry Review, XL (June 1949).
"June 2nd, 1953", Times Literary Supplement, 5 June, 1953,
  p. 358.

ANTHOLOGIES IN WHICH POEMS BY V S-W ARE INCLUDED

Georgian Poetry, Vol. V, ed. E.M. (Edward Marsh) The Poetry Bookshop, London, 1922.
  "A Saxon Song", from *Orchard and Vineyard*
  "Mariana in the North" „   „   „
  "Full Moon" „   „   „
  "Sailing Ships" „   „   „
  "Trio" „   „   „
  "Bitterness" „   „   „
  "Evening" „   „   „
Oxford Book of Modern Verse, ed. W.B. Yeats, Oxford, 1936.
  "Greater Cats", from *King's Daughter*
"On the Lake", „ *Collected Poems*
Modern Verse in English, ed. David Cecil and Allen Tate, London, 1958.
  "On the Lake", from *Collected Poems*
  "A Dream" „   „   „
The Atlantic Book of British and American Poetry, II, ed. Edith Sitwell, London, 1959.
  "The spring was late that year", from *The Land*
Georgian Poetry, ed. James Reeves, Penguin Books, London, 1962.
  "Full Moon", from *Orchard and Vineyard*

FICTION

Work	*Reprinted in*
Heritage, Collins, London, Doran, New York, 1919.	
The Dragon in Shallow Waters, Collins, London, 1921, Putnam, New York, 1922.	
The Heir, Heinemann, London, Doran, New York, 1922 (Short stories).	
Challenge, G. Doran, New York, 1923.	
Grey Wethers, Heinemann, London, Doran, New York, 1923.	
"To Be Let Or Sold", *Morning Post,* 14 December, 1923 (Short story).	
Seducers in Ecuador, Hogarth Press, London, 1924, Doran, New York, 1925.	
The Edwardians, Hogarth Press, London, Doubleday, Doran, New York, 1930.	
"Liberty", *Harper's Bazaar,* October 1930, pp. 44—45, 102, 104. (Short story).	
"The Engagement", *Tatler,* 22 October, 1930, pp. 186 & xiv. (Short story).	
"The Unborn Visitant", *Graphic,* Christmas Number, October, 1930, pp. 22, 23, 34, 36. (Short story).	*Thirty Clocks Strike the Hour.*
All Passion Spent, Hogarth Press, London, Doubleday, Doran, New York, 1931.	
"Elizabeth Higginbottom", *Spectator,* CXLVII (21 November, 1931), 613—4. (Short story).	*Thirty Clocks Strike the Hour.*
The Death of Noble Godavary, Ernest Benn, London, 1932.	*Thirty Clocks Strike the Hour.*
Family History, Hogarth Press, London, Doubleday, Doran, New York, 1932.	
Thirty Clocks Strike the Hour, Doubleday, Doran, New York, 1932.	
"The Strange Adventures of Mr Petherick", *Harper's Bazaar,* April 1933, pp. 28, 29, 92.	

The Dark Island, Hogarth Press, London, Doubleday, Doran, New York, 1934.
Grand Canyon, Michael Joseph, London, 1942.
Devil at Westease, Doubleday, New York, 1947.
The Easter Party, Michael Joseph, London, Doubleday, New York, 1953.
No Signposts in the Sea, Michael Joseph, London, Doubleday, New York, 1961.
"Interlude in Two Lives", *Woman's Own,* 24 March, 1962, pp. 9, 83—89 & 30 March, 1962, pp. 57—69.

NON-FICTION

Knole and the Sackvilles, William Heinemann, London, 1922.
"Why women novelists neglect men", *Daily Express,* 14 January, 1922.
The Diary of Lady Anne Clifford, ed. V S-W with a long preface by V S-W. William Heinemann, London, 1923.
"Fashions in Decoration", *Vogue,* London, April 1924, p. 61.
"On being photographed", *Evening Standard,* 15 May, 1924.
"On friends and relations", *Evening Standard,* 30 May, 1924.
"Mme. Dieulafoy", *Vogue,* London, June 1925, p. 77, 112.
"Travelling in Italy", *Nation and Athenaeum,* XXXVII (Travel Number, 1925), 3—4.
"The Garden and the Oast", *Nation and Athenaeum,* XXXVIII (10 October, 1925), 47—8.
"Gertrude Bell in Bagdad", *Nation and Athenaeum,* XXXIX (24 July, 1926).
Passenger to Teheran, Hogarth Press, London, 1926.
"Gulistan", *Nation and Athenaeum,* XXXIX (10 July, 1926), 413—4.
"Migration", *Nation and Athenaeum,* XLI (25 June, 1927), 411—2.
"Some Tendencies of Modern English Poetry", *Essays by Divers Hands,* VII (1927), Royal Society of Literature, London (Lecture).
Aphra Behn, Gerald Howe, London, 1927, Viking Press, N.Y., 1928.
"The Wit and the Wanderer", *Nation and Athenaeum,* XLIII (16 June, 1928), 358—9 (Article on Dr Johnson and Psalmanazar).
"Strange Adventures", *Time and Tide,* IX (13 July, 1928), 679—80.
"Civilized Subterfuges", *Vanity Fair,* July 1928, pp. 33, 80.
"Tolstoy", *Nation and Athenaeum,* XLIII (8 September, 1928), 729—30.
Twelve Days, Hogarth Press, London, Doubleday, Doran, N.Y., 1928.
"On poetry today", *Radio Times,* 2 November, 1928, pp. 289—90.
"Four English poets of our own time", *Radio Times,* 9 November, 1928, pp. 362—3.
"Modern poetry is not prose", *Radio Times,* 23 November, 1928, pp. 515—6.
"The formidable Mr. Eliot", *Radio Times,* 30 November, 1928, pp. 589, 628.
"The Ukraine", *Life and Letters,* December 1928, pp. 575—9.
"Multitude or solitude?", *Daily Chronicle,* 5 December, 1928.
"The double existence of the Sitwells", *Radio Times,* 14 December, 1928, pp. 728—9.
"There are many fine poets today", *Radio Times,* 18 January, 1929, pp. 127, 130.
"Marriage", *Listener,* I (26 June, 1929), 899—900.
Andrew Marvell, Faber & Faber, London, 1929.
"The Georgians", *Daily Mail,* 14 July, 1930.
"Youth is perplexed", *Daily Mail,* 21 July, 1930.
"The future of the novel", *Week-end Review,* II (October 1930), 535, 537. *Bookman,* N.Y., LXXII (December 1930), 350—1.
"Life in a cloud of ink", *Graphic,* 27 December, 1930, p. 567.
"Women in literature", *Woman's Leader,* XXII (2 January, 1931), 363.
"The Edwardians below stairs", *Vogue,* 25 November, 1931, pp. 55—7.

"Preface" to Walther Berendsohn, *Selma Lagerlöf: her life and work,* trans. George Timson, Nicholson & Watson, London, 1931.

"George Eliot", *The Great Victorians,* ed. Massingham, Nicholson & Watson, London, 1932.

"Memory—good and bad", *Spectator,* CIL (30 July, 1932).

"Ghosts", *Nash's,* December 1932, p. 52.

"Now I am a millionaire", *Nash's,* January 1933, p. 68.

"On being beautiful", *Nash's,* May 1933, p. 5.

"Our future beckons", *Pictorial Review,* XXXV (November 1933), 19, 37.

"On being unpunctual", *Everyman,* 1 December, 1933.

"Elizabethan Lyrics and Metaphysical Poetry", Lord Northcliffe Lectures, 1934. (Six lectures delivered at the University of London; MSS in the possession of Mr Nigel Nicolson, Sissinghurst Castle.)

"V. Sackville-West", *Beginnings,* ed. L.A.G. Strong, Thomas Nelson, London, 1935.

Saint Joan of Arc, Cobden, Sanderson, London, Doubleday, Doran, N.Y., 1936.

Some Flowers, Cobden, Sanderson, London, 1937.

Pepita, Hogarth Press, London, Doubleday, Doran, N.Y., 1937.

"W.H. Hudson: Naturalist and poet", *Listener,* XIX (2 June, 1938), 1193—4.

"Vivisection", *New Statesman & Nation,* XVI (3 December, 1938), 913—4.

Country Notes, Michael Joseph, London, 1939, Harper, N.Y., 1940.

"Hilda Matheson", *Spectator,* CLXV (22 November, 1940).

Country Notes in Wartime, Michael Joseph, London, 1940, Doubleday, Doran, N.Y., 1941.

"Virginia Woolf", *Horizon,* III (May 1941).

English Country Houses, Collins, London, 1941.

"Knole", *Spectator,* CLXXI (15 October, 1943), 356.

The Eagle and the Dove, Michael Joseph, London, 1943, Doubleday, Doran, N.Y., 1944.

"Progress in Persia", *Vogue,* January 1944, pp. 48—9, 67.

"Sharawadji", *Spectator,* CLXXII (14 January, 1944), 29.

"Shepetovka", *Spectator,* CLXXII (25 February, 1944), 169.

The Women's Land Army, Michael Joseph, London, 1944.

"Delight in Gardens", *Listener,* XXXIII (22 March, 1945), 327—8.

"Wordsworth, especially in relation to modern poetry", *Essays by Divers Hands,* XXII (1945), Royal Society of Literature, London (Lecture).

ed. V S-W and Harold Nicolson, *Another World Than This,* Michael Joseph, London, 1945. (Occasional book).

"Introduction" to *Alice Meynell: Prose and Poetry,* ed. F.P., V.M., O.S., & F.M., Jonathan Cape, London, 1947.

Nursery Rhymes, Dropmore Press, London, 1947.

"Gertrude Bell", *Listener,* XL (2 December, 1948), 852—3.

"Bees under my bonnet", *Time and Tide,* XXX (3 December, 1949), 1212.

"A question of inspiration", *New Statesman & Nation,* 21 January, 1950, p. 62 (Article refuting implication of plagiarism).

"Little Flower Book", *Spectator,* CLXXXIV (30 June, 1950), 879—80.

In Your Garden, Michael Joseph, London, 1951.

"Walter de la Mare and 'The Traveller' ", *Proceedings of the British Academy,* XXXIX (1953), 23—36 (Wharton Lecture on English poetry, 1953).

"The personality of Walter de la Mare", *Listener,* IL (30 April, 1953), 711—2.

"Foreword" to Ernest Raymond, *The Brontë Legend: its cause and treatment,* Cassell, London, 1953.

In Your Garden Again, Michael Joseph, London, 1953.

"Landscape of a mind", *Encounter,* II (January 1954). (Article on Virginia Woolf).

"Censor for tiny tots", *Spectator,* CLII (5 February, 1954), 152—3.

More For Your Garden, Michael Joseph, London, 1955.

"Virginia Woolf and Orlando", *Listener,* LIII (27 January, 1955), 157—8.

"Green London", *Time and Tide,* 26 May, 1956, p. 622.

"Little superstitions", *Listener,* LV (14 June, 1956), 802—3.

"A child in the house", *Listener,* LVI (16 August, 1956), 227—9.

Even More For Your Garden, Michael Joseph, London, 1958.

A Joy of Gardening: A selection for Americans, ed. Hermine Popper, Harper, N.Y., 1958.

Daughter of France, Michael Joseph, London, Doubleday, N.Y., 1959.

Faces: Profiles of dogs, (with photographs by Laelia Goehr), Harvill Press, London, 1961, Doubleday, N.Y., 1962.

CRITICAL AND OTHER ARTICLES ON V. S-W IN HISTORIES OF LITERATURE, BOOKS, MAGAZINES AND NEWSPAPERS.

"The lady of a tradition: Miss Sackville-West", Grant Overton, *American Nights Entertainment,* Appleton, N.Y., 1923, pp. 102—18.

"Victoria Sackville-West", S.P.B. Mais, *Some Modern Authors,* Richards, London, 1923, pp. 142—4.

"A novelist and her ancient heritage", J. Fletcher Smith, Boston *Evening Transcript,* 18 August, 1923.

"A woman of letters", A.L. Carvillon, *World's Work,* XLII (August 1923), 221—2.

"V. Sackville-West", W.H. Chesson, *Bookman,* London, February 1924, pp. 243—4.

Elizabeth A. Drew, *The Modern Novel,* Harcourt, N.Y., 1926, pp. 123, 126, 245, 247.

"Celebrities in undress: LXVIII—V. Sackville-West", Beverley Nichols, *Sketch,* 13 July, 1927, p. 64.

"Victoria Sackville-West", H.J. Newbolt, *New Paths on Helicon,* Nelson, London, 1927, pp. 412—3.

"A woman of the day: V. Sackville-West", Winifred Holtby, *Yorkshire Post,* 19 August, 1927, p. 6.

"V. Sackville-West", A.R. Marble, *A Study of the Modern Novel,* Appleton, N.Y., 1928, pp. 120—1.

"The Hon. V. Sackville-West", E.O. Hoppe, *Morning Post,* March 1929.

"Interviews with celebrities: The poet", Joan Grigsby, *Lady,* 6 June, 1929.

"London literary letter", Hugh Walpole, *New York Herald Tribune,* 22 June, 1930.

"V. Sackville-West", Hugh Walpole, *Bookman,* N.Y., September 1930, pp. 21—6.

"V. Sackville-West", ed. Louis Untermeyer, *Modern British Poetry,* Harcourt, N.Y., 1930, pp. 66—7.

"How writers work", Louise Morgan, *Everyman,* 23 October, 1930, pp. 391—2.

"The new writers: XXI—Victoria Sackville-West", J.S. Will, *Canadian Forum,* (1931), p. 462 —3.

"V. Sackville-West", S.J. Kunitz, *Living Authors,* Wilson, N.Y., 1931, pp. 353—5.

"Victoria Sackville-West: Ladies of Letters—I", Mary Craik, *Good Housekeeping,* February 1932, pp. 16—7, 108—9.

"Women Writers Today: Victoria Sackville-West—her exquisite mind and vision", Winifred Duke, *Glasgow Herald,* 27 September, 1932.

"V. Sackville-West", Mario Praz, *La Stampa,* Rome, 5 December, 1934. Reprinted in *Chronache Inglesi,* I (1950—2), Milan, 287—90.

"V. Sackville-West: A poet in a tradition", Richard Church, *Fortnightly,* N.S., CXLVIII (1940), 601—8. Reprinted in Church, *Eight for Immortality,* Dent, London, 1941.

"Englische Dichterinnen I: Victoria Sackville-West", Hans B. Wagenseil, *The Gate,* Bremen, II (1948), 3—6.

"Victoria Sackville-West", Jacques Vallette, *Mercure de France,* 1—III—1949, pp. 423—31.

"V. Sackville-West", *Die Weltliteratur,* ed. E. Trauwallner, Wien, 1951, I, 444.

"V. Sackville-West", Stanley Kunitz, *Twentieth Century Authors,* 1st Suppl., Wilson, N.Y., 1955, p. 857.

"V. Sackville-West", *New Century Handbook of English Literature,* ed. Clarence Bernhart, Appleton-Century-Crofts, N.Y., 1956, p. 956.

"Full-length Portrait of Vita Sackville-West", Aileen Pippett, *Vogue,* CXXVIII (1956), 284—6, S 1.

"V. Sackville-West", Franz Lennartz, *Ausländische Dichter und Schriftsteller unserer Zeit,* Kröner-Verlag, Stuttgart, 1960, pp. 589—91.

"V. Sackville-West", *Dizionario Universale della Letteratura Contemporanea,* ed. Mondadori, Milan, 1961, pp. 294—5.

"Språk och stil i två dikter av Victoria Sackville-West", Augusta Pierce, (unpublished thesis), Stockholm, 1962.

"V. Sackville-West", *Lexikon der Weltliteratur,* ed. Gero von Wilpert, Stuttgart, 1963, I, 1161.

"V. Sackville-West", *Abriss der englischen Literaturgeschichte in Tabellen,* ed. Annemarie Schöne, Frankfurt a.M., 1965, pp. 267—8.

"V. Sackville-West", *Geschichte der englischen und amerikanischen Literatur,* ed. Walter F. Schirmer, 3. Aufl., 1966, II, 299—300.

"V. Sackville-West", *Der Romanführer,* Reklam-Verlag, Stuttgart, 1966, III, 214—6.

"V. Sackville-West", *Lexikon der Weltliteratur im 20. Jahrhundert,* Herder, Freiburg im Br., 1966, II, 831.

Anthony Burgess, *The Novel Now: A student's guide to contemporary fiction,* Faber & Faber, London, 1967, pp. 129—31.

"V. Sackville-West", Nancy MacKnight, (unpublished thesis), Columbia University, New York, 1968.

"An Analysis of *The Garden* by V. Sackville-West", Michael Stevens, (unpublished thesis), University of Uppsala, 1970.

"V. Sackville-West", *Meyers Handbuch über die Literatur,* 2. Aufl., Mannheim, 1970, p. 744.

"V. Sackville-West", *Dictionary of Literature in the English Language,* ed. Myers, Pergamon Press, Oxford, 1970, pp. 391, 745—6.

LIST OF OTHER WORKS QUOTED OR CONSULTED

Altick, Richard D., *Lives and Letters: A History of Literary Biography in England and America*, Knopf, New York, 1965.

Bacquet, Paul, *Un contemporain d'Elisabeth I: Thomas Sackville*, Droz, Genève, 1966.

Bowra, C.M., *The Heritage of Symbolism*, Macmillan, London, 1943 (Papermac 186).

Brewster, Dorothy, *Virginia Woolf*, Allen & Unwin, London, 1963.

Bullough, Geoffrey, *The Trend of Modern Poetry*, Oliver & Boyd, Edinburgh and London, 1949.

Burke's Peerage and Baronetage, London, 1970.

Calmette, Joseph, *Jeanne d'Arc*, Presses Universitaires de France, Paris, 1946.

Campbell, C.S. jnr., "The Dismissal of Lord Sackville", Biographical Footnotes, *Mississippi Valley Historical Review*, XLIV (March 1958), 635—48.

Complete Peerage, The, London, 1910—48.

Cordier, Jacques, *Jeanne d'Arc: sa personalité, son rôle*, Les Editions de la Table Ronde, Paris, 1948.

Cruse, Amy, *After the Victorians*, Allen & Unwin, London, 1938.

Dictionary of National Biography, The, London, 1885—1959.

Dunn, Waldo H., *English Biography*, Dent, London, 1916.

af Enehjelm, Helen, "En litterär vänskap: V. Sackville-West och *Orlando*", *Hemlängtan*, Medéns förlag, Stockholm, 1946.

Fabre, Lucien, *Jeanne d'Arc*, Tallandier, Paris, 1947.

Freedman, Ralph, "Virginia Woolf", *The Lyrical Novel*, Princeton University Press, New Jersey, 1963.

Garraty, John A., *The Nature of Biography*, Jonathan Cape, London, 1958.

Grierson, Herbert & Smith, J.C., *A Critical History of English Poetry*, Chatto & Windus, London, 1944.

Hafley, James, *The Glass Roof: Virginia Woolf as a Novelist*, University of California Press, Berkeley, Cal., 1954.

Hassall, Christopher, *Edward Marsh: A Biography*, Longmans, London, 1959.

Hinckley, T.C., "George Osgoodby and the Murchison Letter", Biographical Footnotes, *Pacific Historical Review*, XXVII (27 November, 1958), 359—70.

Johnstone, J.K., *The Bloomsbury Group*, Secker & Warburg, London, 1954.

Lee, Sidney, *The Principles of English Biography* (Leslie Stephen Lecture), University Press, Cambridge, 1911.

Marder, Herbert, *Feminism and Art*, University of Chicago Press, Chicago, 1968.

MacKnight, Nancy, "V. Sackville-West", (unpublished thesis), Columbia University, New York, 1968.

Nicolson, Harold, *Paul Verlaine*, Constable, London, 1921.

Nicolson, Harold, *The Development of English Biography*, Hogarth Press, London, 1927.

Nicolson, Harold, *Journey to Java*, Constable, London, 1957.

Nicolson, Harold, ed. Nigel Nicolson, *Diaries and Letters, 1930—39*, Collins, London, 1966.

Nicolson, Harold, ed. Nigel Nicolson, *Diaries and Letters, 1939—45*, Collins, London, 1967.

Nicolson, Harold, ed. Nigel Nicolson, *Diaries and Letters, 1945—62*, Collins, London, 1968.

Palmer, Herbert, *Post-Victorian Poetry*, Dent, London, 1938.

Phillips, Charles, *History of the Sackville family, together with a description of Knole and the early owners of Knole*, Vols I & II, Cassell, London, 1930.

Pierce, Augusta, "Språk och stil i två dikter av Victoria Sackville-West", (unpublished thesis in English), Stockholm University, 1962.

Pippett, Aileen, *The Moth and the Star: A Biography of Virginia Woolf,* Little, Brown & Co., Boston, Mass., 1955.

Ross, Robert H., *The Georgian Revolt: Rise and Fall of a Poetic Ideal, 1910—1922,* Southern Illinois University Press, Carbondale, 1965.

Sackville, Victoria Josefa, Lady, MS Diary, in the possession of Mr Nigel Nicolson, Sissinghurst Castle, Kent.

Sackville-West, V., MS Autobiography, in the possession of Mr Nigel Nicolson.

Sackville-West, V., MS Diary, in the possession of Mr Nigel Nicolson.

Spender, Stephen, *World within World,* Hamish Hamilton, London, 1951.

Steegmuller, Francis, *La Grande Mademoiselle,* Hamish Hamilton, London, 1955.

Stevens, Michael, "An Analysis of *The Garden* by V. Sackville-West", (unpublished thesis), University of Uppsala, 1970.

Strong, L.A.G., "English Poetry since Brooke", *The Nineteenth Century and After,* CXVI (1934), 460—8.

Ward, A.C., *Twentieth Century Literature,* Methuen, London, 1945.

Wines, Jean, "A Bibliography of the Writings of Victoria Sackville-West", University of London, Dip. Lib., 1958.

Wolf, John B., "The Reign of Louis XIV: A Select Bibliography of Writings since the War of 1914—18", *Journal of Modern History,* XXXVI (March 1964), 127—44.

Wolf, John B., *Louis XIV,* Gollancz, London, 1968.

Woolf, Leonard, *Downhill all the Way: An Autobiography of the Years 1919 to 1939,* Hogarth Press, London, 1967.

Woolf, Leonard, *The Journey not the Arrival Matters: An Autobiography of the Years 1939 to 1969,* Hogarth Press, London, 1969.

Woolf, Virginia, *Orlando,* Hogarth Press, London, 1928.

Woolf, Virginia, ed. Leonard Woolf, *A Writer's Diary,* Hogarth Press, London, 1954.

Index of Reviews

A selection of the reviews of the works of V S-W consulted during the preparation of this dissertation. The list makes no claim to completeness; it aims rather at providing a representative selection of reviews that have appeared in newspapers and magazines of repute, as well as those which have appeared in less well-known sources if they are of particular interest.
References are to the following newspapers and magazines:

SZ	*Süddeutsche Zeitung*, München.
Ta	*Tagesspiegel*, Berlin.
Ti	*Times*, London.
TLS	*Times Literary Supplement*, London.
WaS	*Washington Star*.
WD	*Weekly Dispatch*, London.
WdL	*Welt der Literatur*, Hamburg.
We	*Welt*, Hamburg.
Ww	*Weltwoche*, Zürich.
Ze	*Zeit*, Hamburg.
Zu	*Zukunft*.

Poems of West and East, MP, 12/10/17; *TLS*, 25/10/17.

Heritage, AthL, 30/5/19; *BmL*, June 1919; *BmN*, June 1919; *BrE*, 25/10/19; *ET*, 27/8/19; *MdF*, 15-VI-1920, p. 818; *MP*, 13/6/19; *NaL*, 14/6/19; *NoA* (?); *Obs*, 18/5/19; *Sco*, 19/5/19; *SuT*, 22/6/19; *TLS*, 22/5/19.

The Dragon in Shallow Waters, DNe, 12/7/21; *Fi* (?); *MdF*, 1-II-1922, p. 808; *NYH*, 13/10/21; *NYT*, 26/3/22; *Obs*, 5/6/21; *Sp*, CXXVII (23/7/21), 115; *TLS*, 16/6/21; *Was* (?).

Orchard and Vineyard, TLS, 1/12/21, p. 791.

The Heir, Bü, Mai—Juni 1949; *DNe*, (?); *DT*, 11/8/22; *FNP*, 9/7/48; *NaN*, CIXX (3/9/24), 250; *N&A*, 24/6/22, p. 436; *LM*, 22/10/22; *NYT*, (?); *Obs*, 18/6/22; *S*, 10/6/22; *Sp*, CXXVIII (24/6/22), 789; *Ta*, 2/8/48; *TLS*, 29/6/22, p. 427.

Knole and the Sackvilles, N&A, 6/1/23, p. 553; *Obs*, 17/12/22; *Sp*, (Lit. Suppl.) 10/2/23, p. 218; *TLS*, 7/12/22, p. 809.

Challenge, BmN, (?); *NYT*, 18/2/23, p. 11.

Grey Wethers, DT, 10/7/23; *N&A*, 28/7/23, p. 552; *NeS*, XXXIX (21/7/23), 448; *Sp*, 11/8/23, p. 197; *TLS*, 23/6/23, p. 438.

Seducers in Ecuador, Ath, Heft 4 (1947); *He*, 1/12/46; *MPW*, 4/4/47; *NYT*, 5/7/25; *TLS* 27/11/24, p. 794; *Zu*, 20/7/47.

The Land, BmL, LXXI (Nov. 1926), 112; *C*, 19/3/27; *DAG*, (?); *FZ*, (?); *MP*, 15/10/26, 17/6/27; *N&A*, XL (6/11/26), 188; *Obs*, Oct. 1926, Dec. 1926; *Sp*, 30/10/26, p. 758; *TLS*, 21/10/26, p. 716; *WD*, 30/1/27.

Passenger to Teheran, N&A, 4/12/26, p. 354; *Sp*, 11/12/26, p. 1081; *TLS*, 4/11/26, p. 758;

Aphra Behn, BmN, LXVII (June 1928), 445; *NaL*, CXXVII (5/9/28), 232; *N&A*, XLII (3/12/27), 360; *NeS* (3/12/27), 250; *NYHT*, 1/4/28, p. 7; *S*, CXLIV (26/11/27), 744; *Sp*, CXXXIX (12/11/27), 836; *TLS*, 24/11/27, p. 856.

Twelve Days, CoL, 10/11/28; *DT*, 9/11/28; *Sp*, CXLI (24/11/28), 781; *TLS*, Dec. 1928.

King's Daughter, BmN, LXXII (Feb. 1931), 649; *JC*, 5/12/29, p. 612; *Sp*, CXLIII (28/12/29), 984; *SuT*, 29/12/29.

Andrew Marvell, Obs, 19/1/30; *Sp*, CXLIII (21/12/29), 956; *TLS*, 17/10/29, p. 813.

The Edwardians, BmN, LXXII (Sept. 1930), 70—1; *BüW*, 29 J (1932), 148; *DN*, 18/11/31, p. 8; *Lit.* 34 J (1931—2), 293; *MaG*, 30/5/30; *NL*, XXXIV (Jan. 1933), 29; *NYT*, 7/9/30, p. 7; *Sa*, VII (13/9/30), 122; *Sp*, CXLVI (30/5/30), 872; *SvD*, 20/8/30; *TLS*, 29/5/30, p. 454.

Augustan Books of Poetry, Sch, 27/8/31.

Sissinghurst, E, 27/8/31; *MaG*, 27/8/31; *SER*, 20/11/31; *Ti*, 13/8/31; *TLS*, 21/9/33, p. 635.

All Passion Spent, BmN, LXXIV (Nov. 1931), 338; *FR*, CXXXVI (July 1931), 132; *Gr*, 26 J (1931—2), 293; *MaG*, 2/6/31; *NS&N*, I (6/6/31), 547; *NYT*, 30/8/31, p. 7; *Sa*, VIII (12/9/31), 116; *Sp*, CXLVII (30/5/31), 872; *St*, 20/9/31; *TLS*, 28/5/31, p. 424.

The Diary of Lady Anne Clifford, TLS, 1931.

Duineser Elegien, Sp. 21/11/31; *TLS*, 6/11/31.

Thirty Clocks Strike the Hour (The Death of Noble Godavary), BmL, July 1932; *Gr*, 27 J (1932—3), 451; *NYT*, 12/6/32; *Obs*, 10/7/32; *TLS*, 7/7/32, p. 501.

Family History, A, CLXV (1934), 305; *BmN*, LXXV (Nov. 1932), 734; *Gr*, 28 J (1933—4), 284—5; *MaG*, 28/10/32; *NS&N*, IV (22/10/32), 490; *NYT*, 30/10/32; *Sa*, IX (31/12/32), 353; *Sp*, CIL (22/10/32), 556; *TLS*, 13/10/32, p. 730.

Collected Poems, BDM, 11/12/33; *MaG*, 12/12/33; *NS&N*, VII (12/5/34), 740; *NYT*, 18/3/34, pp. 2, 15; *Obs*, 26/11/33; *TLS*, 30/11/33, p. 852.

The Dark Island, MaG, 2/11/34; *NS&N*, VIII (1/12/34), 794; *NYT*, 25/11/34, p. 6; *Sa*, XI (24/11/34), 309; *TLS*, 11/10/34, p. 692.

Saint Joan of Arc, BsM, June 1936; *ChT*, 1/6/36; *DN*, 19/7/36; *ES*, June 1936; *Ho*, 36 J, 338—41; *LD*, 88 J, 465; *Lit.*, 39 J (1936—7), 572—3; *Liv*, 10/6/36; *MaG*, 10/7/36, p. 7; *MdF*, 1-IX-1936, p. 424; *NS&N*, XII (18/7/36), 96; *NYT*, 27/9/36, pp. 1, 18; *Obs*, 7/6/36; *Sco*, 11/6/36; *Sp*, CLVI (19/6/36), 1140; *SvD*, 16/10/37; *TLS*, 6/6/36, p. 469.

Pepita, DN, 10/11/38, p. 6; *Lit*, 41 J, 371—2; *MaG*, 2/11/37; *NS&N*, XIV (30/10/37), 695; *NYT*, 12/12/37, p. 9; *Obs*, 7/11/37, p. 11; *Sp*, 19/11/37, p. 24; *SuT*, 14/11/37; *SvD*, 13/11/38; *TLS*, 30/10/37, p. 796.

Solitude, NS&N, 24/10/38; *TLS*, 29/10/38, p. 690.

Selected Poems, TLS, 9/8/41, p. 387.

English Country Houses, TLS, 1/11/41, p. 546.

Grand Canyon, NYHT, 23/10/42; *NYT*, 25/10/42; *Obs*, 8/11/42; *TLS*, 7/11/42, p. 545.

The Eagle and the Dove, CH, 12/11/43, p. 3; *CT*, 31/12/43; *Gu*, 31/12/43; *JW*, 19/11/43; *MaG*, 17/11/43; *NS&N*, XXVI (13/11/43), 319; *NYHT*, 27/2/44; *NYT*, 20/2/44, pp. 3, 16; *Obs*, 26/12/43, p. 3; *Sp*, 19/11/43; *SuT*, 28/11/43; *TLS*, 11/12/43, p. 594.

Another World Than This, NS&N, XXX (15/12/45), 408; *SuT*, 2/12/45.

The Garden, MaG, 31/7/46; *NS&N*, 13/7/46, p. 32; *Obs*, 26/5/46; *Sp*, 31/5/46, p. 564; *TLS*, 15/6/46, p. 285.

Devil at Westease, It, XXXVIII (1955), 33; *NYT*, 11/5/47, p. 31.

Nursery Rhymes, DN, 24/4/51, p. 4; *TLS*, 4/10/47.

The Easter Party, DA, 11/12/54, p. 4; *DN*, 16/2/53, p. 2; *NS&N*, XLV (7/2/53); *NYT*, 15/2/53, p. 4; *Obs*, 25/1/53; *Sp*, CXC (6/2/53), 158; *SvD*, 16/3/53; *SyD*, 23/11/54, p. 8; *TLS*, 6/2/53, p. 88.

In Your Garden Again, TLS, 18/12/53, p. 820.

Daughter of France, MdF, Juillet 1959, p. 527; *NS&N*, LVII (18/4/59), 549; *NYT*, 30/8/59, pp. 7, 30; *NZZ*, 25/11/60; *Obs*, 5/4/59, p. 21; *ILN*, CCXXXIV (1959), 704; *Sp*, 10/4/59, p. 518; *SyD*, 14/8/59, p. 4; *TLS*, 8/5/59, p. 267.

No Signposts in the Sea, B, II (1963), 52; *NvB*, II (1963), 16—7; *Nw* LVII (24/4/61), 66; *NS&N*, LXI (24/2/61), 313; *Obs*, 5/2/61, p. 28; *Sp*, 10/2/61, p. 198; *SZ*, 21/9/63; *TLS* 10/2/61; *WdL*, 25/11/65; *Ww*, 1/4/66.

Faces: Profiles of Dogs, TLS, 22/12/61, p. 919.

General Index